Trends and Issues
in Secondary Education

THE LIBRARY OF EDUCATION

A Project of The Center for Applied Research in Education, Inc.

G. R. Gottschalk, Director

Categories of Coverage

I	II	III
Curriculum and Teaching	Administration, Organization, and Finance	Psychology

IV	V	VI
History, Philosophy, and Social Foundations	Professional Skills	Educational Institutions

38031

Trends and Issues
in Secondary Education

HARL R. DOUGLASS

School of Education
University of Colorado

1962
The Center for Applied Research in Education, Inc.
Washington, D.C.

Foreword

In this brief volume *Trends and Issues in Secondary Education,* Dr. Harl R. Douglass discusses a remarkable number of significant trends which are now occurring. He describes the stirrings and the rumblings that are taking place in secondary schools in this country. For indeed they are many, and the secondary school of today is not what it was even ten years ago. It is not a comfortable place for the traditional high school principal who feels secure only when he holds down change. As Dr. Douglass portrays, these changes include new insights into learner growth; new emphases in subject offerings; radically revised content in some subjects; new instructional media that foretell profound changes in the encrusted "recitation" method; grouping and scheduling that has a flexibility not envisioned a few years ago; the teaming of staff to utilize their potentialities; a new vision of what is needed by the talented and by those handicapped by native endowment, injury, or their neighborhood; and flexible buildings and equipment to accompany some of these changes.

Dr. Douglass includes trends in curriculum, instruction, instructional materials, facilities, guidance, extracurricular activities, school organization, and staff. He has been in a good position to observe these trends in secondary education, for he has visited and been a speaker in hundreds of cities located in every state in the Union except Hawaii and Alaska. His many years of experience have brought him into contact with teachers from every section of the country who have been members of his classes in secondary education. For years he has given a course on "Trends in American Education" with particular reference to secondary education.

In this book Dr. Douglass draws upon his wide experience and knowledge of secondary education, as well as upon a wealth of publications, to point up some of the current issues and controversies, the need to distinguish between genuine quality and form for form's sake, the understanding of basic theory supporting practices, and the danger of accepting the ideas of every innovator who arouses the public. Few are as privileged as Dr. Douglass to speak about secondary education, because few have such a rich background of experience and study of secondary schools in the United States.

VERNON E. ANDERSON
Dean, College of Education
University of Maryland

Contents

ix

*Trends and Issues
in Secondary Education*

CHAPTER I

Conditions Contributing to Trends

The practice of education has been the subject of vigorous controversy in the United States during the past few years. There have been more changes and more proposals for changes and experimentation than in any comparable period.

Recent Criticisms and Proposed Changes

The widest attention has been accorded to various intellectuals —such as Albert Lynd, Arthur Bestor, and Mortimer Smith—who have sharply (and often sensationally) criticized what seemed to them to be a lack of provision, particularly in the area of secondary education, for developing the intellectual traits of young people. These critics were bitterly opposed to what they apparently understood to be progressive education, permissive education, and education for life adjustment. Another, less-informed, group is greatly concerned about the contribution of education to national security. The Soviet Union's launching of Sputnik I and Sputnik II in October 1958 gave rise to an outburst of criticism directed against various phases of secondary education. The deluge of proposals for changes which followed this outburst (not all of which were well thought out) aimed at what the critics apparently thought were low standards of achievement and of study habits in certain areas, particularly science and mathematics.

In the early fall of 1961 James E. Allen, Jr., Commissioner of Education of New York, said that "The rate of instructional innovation in the schools of New York State more than doubled within fifteen months after the launching of Sputnik I."

Better provision for the gifted and the less able. Critics from both groups have argued that more adequate provision should be made for the education of students of superior academic capacity, especially in view of the development of more rigid standards for admittance to institutions of higher education.

1

More recently there has been an aggressive campaign to get schools to recognize young people of very superior potential for creative contributions—especially those who do not achieve well in conventional subjects—and to make better provision for their appropriate education. The increased attention to the education of bright children has stimulated a corresponding concern that the education of the less able students, increasing in number in senior high school years, will not be neglected but improved.

The teacher shortage. The increased enrollment in schools, the trend of college graduates toward positions in industry, and the relatively modest teachers' salaries have combined to produce an acute shortage of teachers. This shortage has in turn given rise to proposals for maximum use of the ablest teachers and for the assignment of teachers to *those* aspects of their fields which they can do best.

Differing conceptions of objectives of education. The controversy over education is augmented by disagreement with respect to the relative importance of the acquisition of information and intellectual skills as compared to the development of ideals, social skills and adaptations, emotional health and personality strength, and other factors making up character.

Quality and excellence. One feature of the recent criticisms of the schools has been the development of a demand on the part of laymen throughout the country for what is coming to be called "quality" education or "excellence" in education. These terms mean different things to different people; indeed, there are many who wish to promote some particular idea or philosophy of education and are referring to it as a means of obtaining "quality" or "excellence." Although the use of these terms without precise definition leads to much confusion and some undesirable exploitation, there is a definite and widespread conviction that the public schools must improve the quality of education which the young people will receive in these days of very unusual demands for well educated people.

Controversy and counter trends. Many of the differences in opinions of those engaged in controversy about American secondary education may be traced to basic differences in the theory and philosophy of secondary education, including such matters as what should be the purposes of secondary education and whether or not secondary education should be obligatory for all young people of appropriate age.

Creativity versus conformity. There has been a greatly increased discussion of the relative place in education of the development of creativity and the development of conformity. Many leading educators are strongly urging that learners be allowed greater opportunity to develop creativity, but there has also been a fairly general demand on the part of the public for the greater exercise of authority—particularly in the matter of discipline—by teachers and school administrators, and for a greater amount of study and homework.

Young people's opposition to conformity is attributed by some careful students of the problem to the traditional desire of youth to avoid conforming to the standards of adult society. Nevertheless young people—whether consciously or unconsciously—have become even greater conformists by repressing their own creativity and individualism, when necessary, in order to win the approval and acceptance of their peers.

Changes and Current Trends in American Life

It is rather generally accepted that the program of the schools must be fluid and flexible in order to keep in harmony with the conditions in American life for which young people are being prepared. To a certain degree, the school programs have always lagged behind the present, probable, and future conditions in life in the United States. Particularly in recent years, living conditions in the United States have undergone a very accelerated rate of change. These new conditions and new trends may be found in every area of living.

Critical changes in homes. The American home has undergone very pronounced changes which have very important implications for programs of the schools. For instance, the number and proportion of divorces and broken homes have greatly increased. The influence of the home on the character and education of young people has been gradually diminishing. More and more mothers work outside the home, and there are more and more parents so busy with their business and social lives that they spend little time at home. A factor contributing to this change has been the stratification of social life on the basis of age level. Also, opportunities or responsibilities for work experience open to young people are not now present in the typical home. Consequently parents are unable to pass on to their young people the valuable knowledge, ideals, and skills previously transmitted from one generation to another. The very presence of television in all but a very small percentage of American homes, has operated to decrease the reliance that may be placed on home study and further to displace the parent-child relationships formerly characteristic of American homes.

Trend toward materialism. Materialism has come more and more to replace the traditional American idealism. In the first place, the virtues of thrift, modesty, and simplicity have given way to the desire for vocational success, material possessions, and recognition through social status and ostentatious display of economic success. Automobiles, clothing, cosmetics, and even the appearance of the home and its furnishings have come to be viewed as indication of economic and social status.

Changes in leisure activities. Another strong trend in recent years has been the shift from simpler leisure pursuits involving home entertainment, reading, and parlor and outdoor games to commercialized amusement of various types including movies, automobile riding, and various forms of amateur and professional athletic contests.

Increase in juvenile delinquency. The statistics of the Federal Bureau of Investigation over the past twenty-five years show a definite and progressive increase in the incidence of crime and delinquency. Although this trend is noticeable at all age levels and in all classes of society, it has in recent years posed a particular problem among adolescents in the slums and crowded sections of the cities, as has been pointed out so forcefully in Dr. Conant's recent book on *Slums and Suburbs*.[1] Especially among the children of such areas, but also generally, the large increase in the number of young

---

[1] James B. Conant, *Slums and Suburbs* (New York: McGraw-Hill Book Co., 1961), 195 pp.

people of secondary school age infected with venereal disease is tragic testimony to changed conditions.

Trend toward softer living. The increase in automatic household appliances has eliminated many of the chores for which young people were formerly responsible. There has also been a strong trend toward softer and easier physical life for young people. The opportunities for gainful employment after school and during vacations have enabled youngsters to satisfy their increased desire for material status symbols. Many are strongly influenced by the example set by cinema heroes and heroines.

The more strenuous types of leisure activities have been displaced by sedentary pursuits. The lack of physical activity among young people in the United States as compared with that of similar age groups in other countries, particularly in Russia, has stimulated much concern. This trend toward a softer life also manifests itself in the schools. For several decades, American boys and girls have tended to use the elective system to avoid the subjects which require more time and effort, and which are least interesting to them. Recently there has been a slight reversal of this trend—no doubt partly attributable to the increased admission requirements imposed by better colleges and the importance attached to high school diplomas by employers.

The increase in population. Philip M. Hauser, Chairman of the Department of Sociology at the University of Chicago (formerly Acting Director of the United States Census Bureau), has pointed out that the population in the United States increased by 48 million people between 1940 and 1960 and will reach 200 million by 1970.[2] Hauser emphasizes that this population explosion is creating a number of very serious problems. These include: (a) lowering the quality of the schools, (b) straining the job market, (c) increasing racial tensions, (d) increasing crime, and (e) creating new slums. Hauser also points out that the Negro population is increasing 60 per cent more rapidly than the white population and that the general trend of the population is from the country to the cities. The consequent development of ghetto-type group living has

---

[2] Philip M. Hauser, "America's Population Increase," *Look*, Vol. 25, No. 24 (November 21, 1961), pp. 30–31; *ibid.* (December 5, 1961), pp. 21–27.

brought with it a severe increase in crime and immorality, and serious problems of transportation and sewage disposal facilities. The solution of these problems will require the understanding and intelligent planning and cooperation of the leaders and all the citizens in our democratic society.

Accelerated developments in technology. The greatly accelerated rate of technological development has increased the productivity of workers and greatly increased the available supply of many types of goods. This has created a problem of readjustment of workers to the demands—demands which have increased in some fields and lessened in others. These developments challenge the traditional economic and legal policies and practices and make it necessary to make appropriate adjustments for business and government which in turn make demands upon the interests and knowledge of the voters and people in general.

Increase in amount of knowledge. The developments in the fields of science and technology and in the fields of economics, sociology, and political science have led to a significant increase in the sum of human knowledge. This constitutes a challenge to reorganization of the subject-matter content in various fields of secondary education as well as at other levels.

There has also been a great increase in the amount of knowledge about the mental, social, and physical and emotional development of human beings. Much of this new knowledge is very pertinent to methods of teaching and various other types of human interpersonal relationships in schools.

More college-bound students.[3] The number and proportion of young people who plan to attend college has very materially increased in the past decade. This increase is partly a result of the so-called "GI Bill" which enabled and encouraged a very large number of young men and young women to go to college who otherwise would not have attended, and partly the result of the increased demand for college graduates. This increase in college-bound students constitutes a definite challenge for better guidance and better preparation of secondary school boys and girls.

---

[3] Whereas in the 1940's the number of students annually attending college was approximately one and a half million, in 1960 it was approximately four million and will no doubt exceed six million in 1970 and seven and a half million in 1980.

Increase in influence of mass media of communication. Not only do more people watch television for longer periods of time, but more people read newspapers, magazines, and books. The control of mass media of communications by a small segment of the population carries the danger that such media may be used for indoctrination. There is always the possibility that—as in Germany, Japan, Italy, Russia, and elsewhere—mass media of communications may be employed to deceive and mislead the citizenry. This strongly suggests the necessity for developing to higher levels the skills of critical reading and listening.

Increased importance of international relations. Important developments in recent years have placed upon the American people a greater responsibility for effective leadership in international relations. Among such developments have been the decline in the sphere of world influence of great democratic powers such as France and Great Britain, the rapid development of the United States and the Soviet Union and its satellites, and China, along with the worldwide movement away from colonialism and toward self-government.

The problem is greatly intensified by the virtual division of most of the world into three groups: the Communist nations, the capitalistic nations, and the growing number of neutral or uncommitted nations, and the strong feeling among the peoples of each of the first two groups that their safety depends upon the defeat of the other by peaceful or forceful means—or both. Added to this is the development of various types of nuclear weapons capable of destruction on such a gigantic scale[4] that nuclear war would most probably mean the annihilation of a majority of the population in the participating countries as well as the means of maintaining life by the survivors.

This situation has been dangerously oversimplified by many Americans who seem to believe that the solution lies merely in the development of a nuclear force superior to that of the Communist nations and in the indoctrination of the American people against Communism. Actually, the most serious race is the struggle be-

---

[4] Leading scientists claim that in 1961 our stockpile of nuclear force is far more than sufficient to destroy all Russians and that the Russians have stockpiled more than sufficient to destroy all Americans.

tween the two factions for the persuasion and allegiance of the large uncommitted groups—particularly in Asia, Africa, and Latin America. The current arms race has been increasingly producing dislocations and dangers in the American economy. There is a great necessity for the education of American citizens along the lines of peace without the sacrifice of their ideas and ideals.

Increased complexity of economic and government problems. The developments in various areas of American life—the population explosion, the advances in technology, the changes in international relations, and the advances in mass communications techniques—seem to point to the necessity for the planning and putting into effect in the schools a program for intelligent citizenship far more effective than that presently obtained in American secondary schools.

Among the more important problems which call for consideration is the danger of depreciating the American gold reserves, the growing political, economic, and social influence of huge business combinations and industrial and labor organizations. Corporations and labor unions have become as powerful and as important a part of American life as the government itself. The presence of this danger calls for the study and understanding of the conditions and principles involved, and the development of ways of protecting the American economy, the interests of the consumer, and the right of equality of opportunity for work in capital investments. The small farmer is gradually disappearing. More and more land is coming under the control of absentee owners of large farms. Over the past twenty-five years, more and more American capital has been invested in foreign countries with all of the complications that are involved including the negative effect upon the balance of trade, the propensity for investors to demand that the American government protect investments abroad, and the weakening of the American dollar.

Also of critical importance is the greatly increased burden of federal taxation, about ten times in 1960 what it was in 1930. The almost unbelievably large government expenditures for development of weapons greatly overshadow the enormous sums that the American people have spent for new school buildings and additional teachers, for urban renewal, and for the welfare of the needy, the aged, and the physically and mentally handicapped. Not only have Federal taxes tripled and quadrupled but state and local taxes more than doubled between 1945 and 1960 and continue to increase.

Greater complication of the problem of relationships between the schools and religion. In recent years a question has arisen over the relationship of the public schools to the teaching of religion and to schools established by religious organizations. The increased prosperity of the American people has enabled more and more parents of all denominations to send their children to schools which charge for tuition and to make gifts, endowments, and bequests to such schools. Partly as a result of these developments, the number of young people attending non-public schools, both elementary and secondary, has greatly increased since 1940.

These developments have naturally led to increased insistence upon a share of public financial support for non-public schools. While this insistence has been spearheaded by Catholic leaders it has also included a mild participation by other Christian educational leaders (although some Protestant sects have opposed the use of public funds for non-public schools).

The increased demand for Federal participation in the support of public schools has focused attention on the question of the extent to which religious values and philosophies should be taught in the public schools. For instance, should Christmas observances in the public schools be carried on in the presence of students of non-Christian faith and children who have not been brought up to believe in any organized form of religion?

"Released time," that is, the excusing of students for an hour or so each week to receive religious instruction elsewhere than in the school, has not proven exceedingly popular either with those with formal religious affiliations or with the teachers and administrators of the public schools. It is clear that such arrangements do not solve the problem. More recently, experimentation with "shared time"—students spending approximately half-time in public and in Catholic schools—is being carried on in a number of metropolitan communities.

A more careful examination of the relationships between the church and the state, and the statement of the position by President Kennedy, has resulted in a general agreement by a large majority of the population that public funds shall not be used for non-public elementary and secondary schools. But the use of public funds for transportation to non-public schools and for school lunches in non-public schools—although it has met with strong resistance in a great majority of American communities—is still an open issue.

Increased Amount and Variety of Experimentation[5]

There has been in the past few years a greatly increased amount and variety of "action research" and controlled experimentation in education. The experiments involve almost every aspect of education—subject requirements, new subject content, different types of school organization, team teaching, the use of teaching machines, language laboratories, measurement and evaluation, grouping and other devices for adapting learning materials and activities to different types of learners especially those of superior and those of inferior academic ability, guidance and counselling, new avenues and techniques of reporting to students and parents, public relations, length of class period, school day, and school year, more independent study by learners, homework acceleration of students through school discussion of controversial issues, use of television, tape recorders and other audio-visual machines and techniques, new types of housing and housing units, programmed textbooks, supervisors, educators and growth of teachers and records.

---

[5] David Mallory in his *New Approaches to Education,* National Council of Independent Schools, describes briefly experiments being conducted in more than two hundred independent schools.

CHAPTER II

Basic Theory and Philosophy

Secondary Education for All

Selectivity in other periods and in other nations. Until about 1920 secondary education, both in the United States and abroad was aimed largely at preparing youngsters for college. Beginning in the early part of this century, enrollments in Grades 7 through 12 (and especially in Grades 10 through 12) in American secondary schools increased very rapidly, moving up approximately from one million above Grade 8 in 1900 to more than ten million in 1961.[1]

In 1961–1962 nearly 90 per cent of the population between the ages of 12 through 17 were enrolled in school. As enrollments have increased, more and more Americans have committed themselves to the philosophy of secondary education for all youngsters. In 1961 there were graduated from the high schools almost two-thirds of those who started with their classes in the seventh grade.

Declining employment opportunities. The greatly increased production per man-hour in many fields of occupations, resulting from advances in technology and increased mechanization has made it possible to produce all the commodities and render all the services needed for a good standard of living without requiring the employment of individuals below the age of eighteen or a work week of not more than 40 hours. These developments, and the tendency to give employment preference to mature workers and those with dependents, has made it increasingly difficult for boys and girls of less than eighteen or nineteen years of age to obtain employment of any kind. In spite of the desire of many boys and girls who are doing poorly in school to leave school for work or marriage, the obvious handicap of wage earners without high school education has augmented the tendency for such boys and girls to stay on in school whether or not they are interested in the subjects taught. Unless

---

[1] Based on figures obtained from the United States Office of Education.

11

and until some agency, such as the Civilian Conservation Camps of the depression years, is instituted, the secondary school will gradually become an educational institution for all young people.

Increasing need for secondary education. The advances in technology have made obvious the need for all young people to obtain more vocational training and/or earlier specialization for this type of world. Similarly, the growing complexity of economic, social, political and international problems clearly calls for intelligent citizenship education as well as a need for wider knowledge and understanding of other peoples. The greatly increased amount of time for leisure and the concomitant trend toward participation in leisure activities which play up sex and violence also call for more education for all Americans.

Increased ability to support education. In the twenty-year period from 1940 to 1960, the average income per person in the United States increased from less than $1,000 to nearly $2,000. In spite of inflationary increases in costs, the American people have been able to support education more and more generously: indeed, the annual cost of all types of schools and colleges in the United States increased from a little more than four billion dollars during 1940 to approximately twenty billion dollars in 1961 (eighteen billion being spent on education in elementary and secondary schools). Even with greatly increased expenditures for defense and other types of expenditures the standard of living of the American people has definitely increased throughout the years. Expenditures for luxuries of various kinds—including sports, travel, cosmetics, and liquor—have increased even more greatly.

Learner Growth and Educational Objectives

Learner growth and subject-matter mastery. Although the importance of subject matter in the educational program has not been questioned, there has been a definite trend in recent decades toward regarding subject matter as a means, not an objective, for stimulating experiences of learners which will result in growth toward desired and envisaged objectives.

Throughout the 1950's, particularly in the latter part of the decade, there developed in many communities a reactionary trend in the direction of educational programs and procedures which emphasize a greater degree of mastery of the subject matter—particularly science, mathematics, foreign languages, American history—by secondary school pupils.

Social, physical, moral, and emotional growth. Although teachers have always recognized the importance of contributing to the desirable moral, social, and emotional development of young people, until recently little attention had been given to the study of how best it might be done and what part teachers in the various subject fields should play in developing young people along those lines. In the last half-century, the increased knowledge about the psychology of human growth has focused much more attention on these types of growth, along with an increased emphasis upon the development of intellectual skills—such as reasoning, critical reading, and creative expression—thus reducing the emphasis upon acquisition of detailed, factual information.

In the past few years more importance has been attached to the training of young people in the intellectual skills, habits and attitudes necessary for effective decision-making. In all areas of life activities, the individual is confronted daily with the necessity for making decisions—many of which are important both with respect to the happiness and well-being of the individual, also of the well-being of the local community, state, nation, and world.

Concomitant growth outcomes. Increasing recognition is being given to the fact that young learners have incidental experiences in school which influence their growth. The learner's experiences—coming into the classroom and participating in classroom activities, receiving approbation or disapproval for his achievement, achieving success or failure in varying degrees, and associating with his schoolmates—will contribute to the acquisition of information and understanding, and to the development of various types of social, physical, and intellectual skills and habits, and a great variety of interests, ideals, and attitudes. Classroom learning activities and other experiences of the young learner are coming to be more frequently planned so as to avoid undesirable growth outcomes such as lack of self-confidence, lack of interest in school and school subjects, attitudes toward school and adult authority in general, and attitudes toward his parents and classmates.

Preparation for areas of life activities. Over the past half-century, attention has focused upon preparation for various areas of life in the determination of the contents and procedures of education. This approach to thinking about the purposes of education (documented by the statement of the goals of education in "The Cardinal Principles of Secondary Education"[2]) has come to characterize the fundamental philosophy of the great majority of teachers and administrators and even of the majority of parents and other laymen. Recent statements of the objectives of secondary education almost invariably include the premise that education should be directed toward effectiveness in earning a living, in home living, in leisure pursuits, in responsibilities of citizenship, in maintaining and improving physical health, and in continued learning.

Although certain subjects make greater and perhaps unique contributions to education for each of these areas, there has been a growing recognition that learning materials and activities should be planned in *all* subjects so as to help prepare the student for happy and effective living.

Teaching as a Professional Art

Prior to the middle of the first quarter of this century, teaching was thought of as (although not by educators) more or less a skilled trade, in which one with a competent store of knowledge developed skill for assigning lessons, making explanations, doing remedial work and testing. In the 1920's and 1930's there was a growing tendency for education to be thought of as a science. Numerous individuals believed that within a few decades education would really become a social science based upon objectively established scientific knowledge.

But there have always been those who emphasized the philosophical aspects of education and maintained that the outstanding feature of an educator is the possession of the sound philosophy of the nature of education and its objectives.

It has become increasingly evident that the teacher acts as a di-

---

[2] A Report of the Committee on the Reorganization of Secondary Education, appointed by the National Education Association, Bulletin, 1918, No. 35, Bureau of Education.

rector of learning activities in the classroom. Although he calls upon his store of available scientific knowledge and upon his knowledge of young people and how they learn, the teacher really performs much as an artist who uses whatever materials and procedures may seem to contribute best to realizing the goals or images he has in mind.

Every minute and every situation in a classroom is to some extent a novel one. General rules must be adapted to a variety of factors, including the particular students—their interests, capabilities, backgrounds—and the teacher himself—his previous experience and what he brings to the classroom. Education is coming to be thought of as an art based upon a sound fundamental philosophy of its nature and objectives, of its relationship to society, knowledge of available subject matter, knowledge of the individual students within the class, and the knowledge of the principles of human growth in general.

Motivation of Learner Participation

Extrinsic versus intrinsic needs. With more and more children going on through secondary schools, and with the increased attractiveness of activities outside the school the problem of stimulating interest in appropriate learning activities has become more significant and pressing. It has been observed that young people in secondary schools in other countries seem to be better motivated and spend much more time in study than young people in the United States.

In the past few years in the United States there has been continued emphasis upon setting up learning activities which are for the most part somewhat interesting and purposeful and that will lead students to spend time and effort on educational growth that will enable them to meet important life needs, including preparation for and success in college.

Immediate versus deferred needs. There has been a corresponding trend toward increased ingenuity on the part of textbook writers and instructors and teachers to organize learning activities so as to meet the felt needs of young people.

Specific versus generic needs. Throughout the past half century there has been a clear trend toward less reliance upon punishment and artificial rewards—such as high marks and favorable comments for hard working students and better achievers, and low marks and unfavorable comments for those achieving less and supposedly less willing to exert themselves. Instead, attention has been focused upon studying for specific needs such as improving speech, improving possibilities for vocational success, and improving capacity for enjoying wholesome leisure and effective home living.

Through the 1930's and 1940's there was a definite trend away from the emphasis upon competition between individuals, particularly under conditions where individuals were "mismatched," that is, unequally prepared to compete. This trend has been criticized quite severely by many of those whose thinking about education was somewhat conservative and particularly by those who are enthusiasts about athletic competition.

Trend Toward an Eclectic Philosophy

Although it is impossible to obtain general agreement on a definite and explicit statement of philosophy of education, the overall trend in a basic philosophy of education held by Americans might well be summarized as follows:

1. Secondary education must be planned for all young people of secondary school age.

2. The major allegiance of public schools must be to the society, to the American nation and people, benefiting individuals as much as they can, but largely through contributions to the common welfare.

3. Subject matter must be selected and organized with a view to its possible contribution to stimulating and guiding learner's experiences which will result in desired growth.

4. Effective educational programs must be developed with a view to providing all types of learner growth—including social, physical, moral, and emotional and intellectual growth—although from day to day the emphasis will be upon intellectual growth with careful consideration of the possibilities of concomitant development of other types of growth.

5. Appeal should be made to a variety of types of motivation involving not only the student's interests in learning activities at

hand but definite recognition of the usefulness of the types of growth to which the learning activities at the time are directed. Less reliance should be placed upon the appeal to general needs wherever these may be replaced by more easily identified specific needs. The possibility of contribution to those needs may be more thoroughly established by research.

BIBLIOGRAPHY

Bryan, A. H., "Reorganization of Our High School Objectives," *Bulletin of the National Association of Secondary-School Principals,* No. 251 (December, 1959), pp. 110–12.

Conant, James B., *The American High School Today.* New York: McGraw-Hill Book Co., 1961, 128 pp.

Educational Policies Commission, *The Contemporary Challenge to American Education.* Washington, D.C.: National Education Association, 1958, 32 pp. Statistics on education in the U.S. and in the USSR: *The Central Purpose of American Education* (1961), 21 pp.

Gruhn, W. T., "Major Issues in Junior High School Education," *The Bulletin of the N.A.S.S.P.,*[3] No. 266 (September, 1961), pp. 19–25.

———, "What Is New in Junior High School Education?" *The Bulletin of the N.A.S.S.P.,* No. 253 (February, 1960), p. 6.

Lambert, Sam M., "Investing in Quality Education," *Phi Delta Kappan,* Vol. XLIII, No. 3 (December, 1961), pp. 110–18.

Orton, Don A., "Issues Raised by Changes in Secondary Education," *The School Review,* Vol. 69, No. 1 (Spring, 1961), pp. 1–11.

Thayer, V. T., *The Role of the School in American Society.* New York: Dodd, Mead & Co., 1960, 520 pp. See Part II, "Changes in the Economic Social Status of Youth," and Part IV, "Critical Issues in Contemporary Education."

Tracy, J. P., "Issues in Catholic Secondary Education," *Catholic School Journal,* Vol. 60 (September, 1960), pp. 46–7.

---

[3] Throughout this volume the letters N.A.S.S.P. will be used to designate the National Association of Secondary-School Principals.

CHAPTER III

Curriculum Offerings, Organization, and Administration

Changes in Offerings and Relative Emphases

Increased emphasis upon science, mathematics, and language. The rate of development of science and technology has been rapidly accelerated over the last quarter of a century, emphasizing the necessity for providing more up-to-date science education for the masses as well as for training scientists and technologists who would conduct research and apply findings to industry, medicine, home life, and to defense.

Since the middle 1950's there has been a growing feeling on the part of a great majority of Americans that more and more of the students should be enrolled in some course in science, in mathematics, and in a foreign language[1] and that those of special aptitudes should not only take more courses in these fields but should be stimulated to a greater degree of achievement in courses developed along modern lines.

This trend has been impeded by the fact that there was a great shortage of science teachers and a slight shortage of mathematics and foreign language teachers. Furthermore, the specialized preparation of many science teachers was limited and somewhat out of date, and the methods of teaching foreign language employed by many teachers were not very effective.

In recent years, largely through government grants under the National Defense Education Act (passed in 1958) and private grants from the educational foundations, there have been institutes established with scholarships for teachers of physical science, biological science, mathematics, and foreign languages.

---

[1] In 1960–1961 nearly two million or approximately 20 per cent of all students in Grades 9–12 were enrolled in a course in a foreign language.

These developments have made it quite clear that there should be two or more versions of courses in mathematics and science for groups of students of definitely different capacities, interests, and future needs in these fields. Despite the shortage of teachers, there has been an annual increase of the number of students enrolling for subjects in these fields. In more and more schools additional foreign languages—notably Russian—are being added.

There has also been an observable trend toward more attention to training in reading in secondary schools. By 1961, a course in reading was offered in the majority of senior high schools.

Trends in education for home living and leisure. As education has come more and more to be viewed as preparation for effective participation in various areas of life including home life, there has been a slight but observable trend in increasing the offerings, although almost always on an elective basis, in education for home living. Furthermore, in a number of subjects—particularly in mathematics, science, and social studies—somewhat more attention has been given to education for home living, including home finance, home management and decoration, marital relations, and rearing of children. This trend has slowed down somewhat in recent years, but increased incidence of juvenile delinquency and divorce and other evidences of the weaknesses in American home life emphasize the need for better education for home living.

Other recent developments in American life have indicated the necessity for a more definite and effective program of education for leisure. At the opening of the century, the average work week was 60 hours; by 1960 the average actual work week was approximately 40 hours with convincing evidence that it would continue to decrease in the future. The ways in which the increased leisure is spent by the great majority of people give reason for alarm. The American public participates to an unprecedented and increasing degree in social drinking and gambling. Many spend their time watching movies or television, in both of which sex and violence have become predominant. The recent trend toward better preparation for leisure involves education for the improvement of tastes in television and movie programs, for appreciation of literature and music of "middle brow" level, development of interests and skills in the various "do-it-yourself" crafts, and in reading along the lines of modern science and economic, political, social, and international events.

Trends in work experience and education for vocation. For more than half a century, there has been a trend to provide work experience as a part of the program of public secondary schools. As the number of young people of less than average intellectual interest and capacity has increased in senior high schools, a tendency to provide programs of work experience in which the student might spend (in addition to his classes in school) eighteen to twenty-four hours a week at work. Getting under way in the 1930's, the distributive education (salesmanship) and diversified occupations programs have spread slowly but steadily.

Provision has also been made in an increasing number of schools —particularly those in which a large percentage of the youngsters are going on to college—for another type of work experience: voluntary civic work participation in school and in the community. From this the youngster not only acquires some skill and knowledge but also develops an interest in and a sense of responsibility for civic progress.

It has been increasingly recognized that vocational training for a large percentage of youngsters cannot be carried out through the conventional vocational subjects. A considerable percentage of young people in every high school will go neither to college nor into occupations for which specific training can be given in the school. Consequently, more attention is being given in English, social studies, mathematics, and science to possible applications and general uses in a considerable number of vocations. Indeed, employers have come to view training in elementary science and mathematics as more important than vocational training.

In 1960 one in every four high school students enrolled in subsidized vocational education courses was studying trades and industries; one in five, agriculture; two in five, home economics; the rest were in work experience programs—diversified occupations or distributive education.

It is interesting to note that since 1959 the secondary school programs in the Soviet Union have begun to provide work experience and work training of all secondary school students—even those who plan to go on to college, a practice which might well be emulated in the United States.

Spread of driver education. Encouraged by the opinions of traffic experts and the substantial decrease in cost of automobile insurance, a large and steadily increasing number of senior high schools now offer courses in driver education. Many of these courses carry credit toward graduation—usually a one-half year unit. By 1959–1960, 72 per cent of all urban schools were offering full facilities for driver education.[2]

Increased emphasis on the social studies. There has been an increasing recognition of the necessity for training future voters for intelligent participation in democratic processes. Many educators are beginning to think that there is an overemphasis upon science and foreign languages and have been arguing very vigorously for more attention to social studies, particularly in the field of economics. As a result of this increased attention, the proportion of students enrolled in social studies classes—which had fallen in the middle 1950's—have begun to increase.

As the result of current international problems, more attention is being given to the history and the cultures of the people of Asia, Latin America, Africa, and the Soviet Union. Many schools have added a course in world geography which surveys the economic, cultural, and governmental characteristics of various countries.

Increased attention to physical and health education. Because so many young people lack adequate physical activity, and because the performance of boys and girls in the United States does not compare favorably with that of similar age groups in other countries (particularly the Soviet Union), much more attention has been given in the past few years to a more vigorous physical and health education program for the secondary schools. The only real evil of "spectatoritis" on the part of boys and girls of secondary school age lies in the fact that they are content to lead a very sedentary life. The availability of public transportation to and from the school and the abundance of automobiles (many youngsters beyond the age of sixteen drive to school) has no doubt added to the situation which many educators think ought to be corrected.

---

[2] *N.E.A. Research Bulletin,* 39 (February, 1961), p. 29.

In 1961, President Kennedy suggested the following program for developing youth fitness:

1. Provide for each pupil a complete physical appraisal, including a battery of tests that have a validated standard of performance for each test item.

2. Provide a developmental program based on individual deficiencies and needs.

3. Reorient existing physical education and recreation programs in the direction of developing general physical fitness.

4. Permit no substitution of military training, athletic training or competition, or other student co-curricular activities for physical education instruction.

5. Require physical education instruction for a minimum of 30 minutes per day, five days each week, for grades one through six; and one standard class period per day, five days per week, for pupils in grades seven through twelve.

6. Provide regular and progressive instruction in health and safety education by qualified teachers.

7. Utilize the health resources of official and voluntary agencies and professional groups within the community.

8. Provide sports and fitness clubs and intramural sports for all young people so that they can participate and compete in the various activities learned in physical education.[3]

Increased emphasis upon sex education. Increased attention has been given in recent years to more adequate sex education in the schools. The growing emphasis in movies and television on sex and sex relations, the constantly rising number of unmarried mothers, illegitimate children, precipitate weddings, and divorces as well as the alarming increase of venereal disease since the 1950's, has weakened the opposition of those who formerly opposed sex education.

Trends in Curriculum
Organization and Administration

The elective system and subjects required for graduation. The elective system was developed in the early part of this century and spread widely as a means of providing for students of various capabilities, interests, and needs. But one of the evils of the elective

---

[3] "President's Program for Youth Fitness," *California Schools* (September, 1961), pp. 358–59.

system as operated in the large majority of secondary schools was that students were able to graduate with significant gaps in their education—for example, in the areas of science, mathematics, social studies, and written expression.

In recent years more and more secondary schools have come to require at least two years of some form of science, two years of mathematics, and three years of social studies, beyond the eighth grade.[4] This has necessitated a development of at least two "tracks" or types of courses in these fields to provide for groups of students with different academic capabilities and interests. In many schools with classroom periods of 55 minutes or more, classes usually meeting five times a week meet only four times—thus avoiding the necessity for employing additional teachers and enabling students carrying five and one-half to six units of work to schedule their programs. There has been a definite trend toward requiring for graduation that at least eleven year-units of credit above the eighth grade be earned in the fields of English, history and the social studies, science, and mathematics, and that they be distributed over these four fields.

Types of curriculum organization. Since the beginning of this century, most secondary schools have offered more than one curriculum. These curricula were organized on the basis of the subjects included—for example, a science college preparatory curriculum, a classical college preparatory curriculum, an English curriculum, and a home economics curriculum.

In the 1920's, stimulated by the introduction of courses in business, agriculture, auto mechanics, and other vocational fields, curriculum organization began to be based on the student's interest and

---

[4] Conant in his *The American High School* (McGraw-Hill Book Company, Inc., 1959) recommended the requirement of four years of English, three or four units of social studies (including two years in history and one on American social problems or American government in the senior year), one year of mathematics (algebra or general mathematics), and at least one year of science (which might well be biology or general physical science). The author of this volume has for many years recommended a similar program with the following modifications: that two units of mathematics (algebra and geometry or two years of general mathematics—one in the junior or senior year), two years of social studies, and two years of science be required in schools in which there are at least two tracks for the abler and less able academically, and that provision be made for gifted students to be excused from not more than two of the required units upon the strong recommendation of a counsellor.

future needs—for example, a college preparatory curriculum, a secretarial curriculum, an auto mechanics curriculum, a household arts curriculum, and a general education curriculum.

In the past few years the extension and improvement of counselling and guidance services in secondary schools has given use to a trend toward a single curriculum comprised of required and elective subjects. The student, with the help and approval of a counsellor, may work out an individual curriculum for himself. Many of the schools offering this single curriculum suggest arrangements of recommended subjects comparable to the older multiple-curriculum type of organization.

The core and unified studies plan. The trend—begun in the 1920's—to break down the barriers between subjects and to teach them in relation with one another, continues at a somewhat slower pace. This is the concept underlying the "core" curriculum. More than 60 per cent of the junior high schools offer the "core" or unified studies plan in some form. In senior high schools the movement is not spreading observably, although interrelated courses in different fields of mathematics, different fields of science, and different fields of social studies are offered.

Most authorities in the field agree that "core" merely involves organizing two or more subjects around problems—particularly problems which constitute felt needs of the learners. In actual practice, even where the interrelated subject, large "block" plan is called the core curriculum, it often involves only English and social studies. Although a few schools were tempted to include more than two subjects in the core area—for example, mathemathics, science, and English, or English, social studies, and science—the trend in this direction has spent itself without having gone far. The trend toward team teaching is tending to break down subjects into distinct parts rather than to combine them into related wholes.

A national curriculum? In recent years, Professor Paul Hanna of Stanford University and others have advocated a national curriculum to be used at least on an advisory basis by all of the schools of the United States. Some thirty-odd years ago, H. G. Wells, in his *Salvaging Civilization,* advocated that a national curriculum and a standard system of instructional methods be employed. Teachers would thus be supplied with, if not compelled to use, the best "materials" and the best "methods." There is little likelihood that this proposal will get much beyond the stage of recommendation. Yet it has some merit: curriculum revision—with respect to the subjects taught, the subjects required, and the content of subjects— is always far behind the needs of today, to say nothing of those of tomorrow. To leave to the individual schools and teachers the problem of bringing the curriculum up to date seems almost hopeless. Furthermore, the increased and sometime uninformed concern about juvenile delinquency and sex immorality and anticommunist hysteria has in recent years heightened the pressure exerted upon the schools by local groups and individuals with narrow and specialized points of view. However, since different individual learners require different learning materials and activities, the idea of a national curriculum has very formidable limitations.

Terminal curricula. Students who will not complete high school, and those who will complete high school but will not go on for further education, require a curriculum made up of subjects which will fit their needs in life. The need for such a curriculum has been the subject of much discussion and considerable practice in recent years. Not only the subjects offered, but also their content and presentation, must be adapted to the needs of the terminal student.

BIBLIOGRAPHY

Baughman, Dale, "Special Reading Instruction in Junior High Schools," *The Clearing House,* Vol. 35 (March, 1961), pp. 394–97.

Bauman, Henry A., Ursula Hogan, and Charles C. Greene, *Reading Instruction in the Secondary School.* New York: Longmans, Green & Co., Inc., 1961, 266 pp.

Becker, James M., "Education for Participation in World Affairs," *The Bulletin of the N.A.S.S.P.,* No. 258 (September, 1960), pp. 143–50.

Brown, Kenneth E., and S. Osbourn Ellsworth, *Offerings and Enrollments in Science and Mathematics in Public High Schools.* Washington, D.C.: U.S. Office of Education, 1958, 87 pp.

Conant, James B., "Recommendations for the Junior High School," *Education Digest,* Vol. 25, No. 4 (December, 1960), pp. 5–9.

——, *The American High School Today.* New York: McGraw-Hill Book Co., 1959, 140 pp.

"Foreign Language Instruction in Secondary Schools," *California Schools,* Vol. 33 (February, 1962), pp. 37–47.

Green, J. J., "Some Ideas About the Secondary School Curriculum," *National Catholic Education Association Bulletin,* Vol. 52 (February, 1956), pp. 18–26.

Handlin, Oscar, "Live Students and Dead Education," *The Atlantic Monthly,* Vol. 208, No. 3 (September, 1961), pp. 29–34.

Hunt, DeWitt, "Work Experience Education Programs in American Secondary Schools." U.S. Department of Health, Education and Welfare *Bulletin,* No. 5 (Washington, D.C.: U.S. Department of Health, Education and Welfare, 1957), 94 pp.

"International Understanding Through the Secondary School Curriculum," *The Bulletin of the N.A.S.S.P.,* No. 224 (December, 1956), pp. 9–164.

Jackson, Arthur, "A Program for the Education of Negro Youth," *The Negro Educational Review,* Vol. IX (July, 1958), pp. 111–16.

Keller, Charles R., "The Twelfth-Grade Problem," *The Bulletin of the N.A.S.S.P.,* No. 264 (April, 1961), pp. 342–49.

Kostbaden, J. and J. M. Ball, "Geography and Education for Citizenship," *The Bulletin of the N.A.S.S.P.,* No. 253 (February, 1960), pp. 159–65.

Marland, S. P., Jr., "Placing Sex Education in the Curriculum," *Phi Delta Kappan,* Vol. XLIII, No. 3 (December, 1961), pp. 132–35.

Mott, Kenneth, "Language Arts—Social Studies Fusion in the Junior High School Block Period," *The Bulletin of the N.A.S.S.P.,* Vol. 44, No. 66 (March, 1960), pp. 124–31.

National Commission on Safety Education, *Driver Education and Driving Simulators.* Washington, D.C.: National Education Association, 1960, 72 pp.

Tally, Ann M., "Art Education in the Secondary School," *The Bulletin of the N.A.S.S.P.,* No. 263 (March, 1961), pp. 1–102.

U.S. Department of Health, Education and Welfare, Office of Education, "Financial Assistance for Strengthening Science, Mathematics, and Modern Foreign Language Instruction," *REGULATIONS,* Sections 301 through 304 of Title III, National Defense Education Act of 1958. Washington, D.C.: U.S. Government Printing Office, 1960.

Wiles, Kimball, and Franklin Patterson, *The High School We Need.* Washington, D.C.: National Education Association, Association for Supervision and Curriculum Development, 1959, 32 pp.

World Geography Bibliography. Albany, N.Y.: Bureau of Secondary Curriculum Development, University of the State of New York, State Education Department, 1961, 80 pp.

Wright, Grace S., *Block-of-Time Classes and the Core Program in the Junior High School.* U.S. Office of Education Bulletin No. 6. Washington, D.C.: Government Printing Office, 1958, 66 pp.

——, *Requirements for High School Graduation in States and Large Cities.* Washington, D.C.: U.S. Office of Education, 1961, 34 pp.

CHAPTER IV

Content of Subjects Offered

Relationship to Life Situations

Parents have always demanded that school work be more closely related to life situations and life needs. Even as far back as 1748, Benjamin Franklin so forcefully put himself on record as being in favor of such a development. In his autobiographical book, *The Education of Henry Adams,* the author complained that his education had prepared him to live in the time of Julius Caesar.

Education for life adjustment. Out of this demand has grown the vast area of vocational subjects, but there has remained a general desire for the nonvocational subjects—English, science, mathematics, and history—to be taught in closer connection with life situations which the learners were almost certain to face. This is the concept behind education for life adjustment.

In recent years there have developed (partly aided by audio-visual aids of various kinds) courses of study and methods of teaching which relate learning activities to situations in personal and community life relationships. Science too is coming to be taught in relationship to current life problems, not only those involving nuclear fission and air and space, but also to everyday problems in the fields of health and of sex. These developments have been slow and difficult, because so many "well-prepared" teachers have little knowledge of life applications of their subjects—and indeed of life situations in general.

Because there is less need for training in home economics, courses in this field are being revised: less attention is being given to the preparation of foods and to sewing and much to such topics as nutrition, health in the home, clothing repair, consumer and business education, and personal relations in the home (including not only marital relations, but also child-parent relations).

Moral and spiritual education materials. Partly as a result of the general alarm at the great increase in divorce, crime, juvenile delinquency, and dishonesty in business, labor organizations, and government, there is a tendency to give increased attention to the teaching of moral and spiritual values by teachers of all subjects, especially by those of social studies and literature.[1]

Community resources. There is also the trend toward the use of community resources in instruction; this of course involves field trips and excursions, but it also involves the use of persons who may be interviewed or who may be brought into the classroom to explain some phase of a particular problem or subject.

Content Organization

Large units. For more than thirty years there has been a trend toward the organization of learning materials and activities in units larger than daily assignments. The percentage of teachers employing large units—particularly in the field of English, science, history and social studies, and health education—is growing slowly but steadily.

Resource units. Courses of study are coming to be supplemented or replaced with "resource units." A resource unit is a reservoir of plans and materials for teaching a large unit of a subject which includes suggestions for the use of textbooks, supplementary materials, audio-visual aids, student activities, culminating activities, testing and evaluation, and so on. The teacher is expected to formulate his own unit with the help of these suggestions.

Purposeful study and community school plans. Another, less pronounced, trend has been the attempt to organize a considerable part of instruction in what may be called "purposeful study," in which the learner's activities in a particular subject have a definite objective—such as providing something for the community, constructing something useful, or rendering some service to the school or to the community.

The trend toward the development of "community schools" was strong in the 1930's but has tended to taper off. There are very few communities in which the school curriculum may be centered

---

[1] In Florida, for example, a guide for teaching moral and spiritual values has been adopted and distributed in the state. The guide stresses such attributes as honesty, integrity, and courage. A dozen pilot schools in Florida have tested the program and have reported favorably.

around community activities whereby the learners and the adults cooperate in the improvement of community life.

Individual and group projects. Another trend, begun in the 1920's, involves the setting up of assignments or the organization of student learner activities around definite goals. Such a unit of learning (now called a "project") covers at least several days and its results are usually tangible rather than the acquisition of information or skill.

With the growing desire of adolescents to work together in peer groups, there has been a trend (particularly in schools which use long periods) to assist young people in the class to organize into subgroups to study together and particularly to work upon group projects. Frequently, different responsibilities are assigned to different individuals in the group and some accomplishment of the group is presented to the entire class.

The block and gap approach. For the past fifteen or twenty years there has been a trend toward emphasizing certain units or portions of a semester or year's course of study and rapidly skimming or omitting altogether other sections of the course. This method is most often employed in history and science courses. Advocates seek to justify it by pointing out that certain topics require intensive treatment and involved rather than superficial acquaintance.

Curriculum Adaptation
for Special Student Groups

The talented and the college-going group. There has been a pronounced trend, particularly since the middle of the 1950's (see Chapter V) toward developing the full learning potential of students with superior academic and intellectual capacity. In many schools this has taken the form of attempting to make better provision for those of the college-going group who are finding it more difficult to gain admission into and to succeed in the colleges of greater national reputation and higher academic standing.

More Audio-Visual Materials

Types of films. There has long been a trend, accelerated in the 1950's, to the use of more audio-visual materials. As listed and defined by DeKieffer and Cochran (see Chapter IV), there have been and are being developed historical films, documentary films, how-to-do-it films, scientific films, appreciation films, personal and social adjustment films, informational films, guidance films, pacing or drill films, story-telling films, recreational films, industrial or promotional films, propaganda films, news and current events films, and professional (education) films.

Particularly useful in large classes is the overhead projector, which enables the instructor to present a largely magnified picture of some object or diagram, or map, and permits him to point out important details.

Far less costly and almost as suitable for average-size classrooms is the eight millimeter film, both with sound and without. The recent trend is toward the use of eight millimeter instead of sixteen millimeter sound track films. Many teacher training institutions and school systems are building libraries of eight millimeter films.

Tape recordings. The substantial decrease in the cost of tape recordings since 1960 has led to their increased use in the secondary schools—not only in such fields as foreign languages, music, speech, and English, but in practically all subjects. Many of the institutions devoted to teacher education have large collections of useful tape recordings in every subject which may be purchased or rented at low cost, and many school systems are forming their own library of tape recordings. Because of the low cost and availability of tape recordings, and because they may be used in undarkened rooms, their value to the schools is growing and will probably continue to grow for some time to come.

Television. Beginning with the early 1950's, there has been a definite trend toward the greater use of television in the schools. The use of local television broadcasts including closed circuits has developed slowly but definitely. In 1961, more than 30 per cent of urban school districts made substantial use of programmed television instruction and perhaps nearly all of the others made some use of it.[2]

Perhaps about half of the large high schools have been wired for closed circuit television although a small fraction of these were

------

[2] Computed from data in *N.E.A. Research Bulletin No. 39* (February, 1961), p. 29.

actually using it in 1962. Regardless of the enthusiastic claims made by optimistic proponents of educational television, it is clear that its use, because of the technological difficulties involved, will develop only very slowly.

Locally constructed materials. Although much farther along in elementary schools than in secondary schools, there has been an increased use of locally constructed visual materials of a greater variety of types including mock-ups, charts, maps, and various kinds of posters.

More Modern Material

Science and mathematics. In recent years there has been a very serious effort (assisted in some instances by generous grants from educational foundations) to improve the content of a number of the subjects in the secondary school curriculum. National and institutional committees have been appointed to work out suggested, improved courses of study in the fields of mathematics, biology, physics, and chemistry. Among these are the following:

MATHEMATICS

1. Commission on Mathematics of the College Entrance Examination Board.
2. Secondary School Curriculum Committee of the National Council of Teachers of Mathematics.
3. The University of Illinois Committee on School Mathematics.
4. The School Mathematics Study Group, Stanford University.
5. The University of Maryland Mathematics Project (junior high school level).
6. Ball State Teachers College Mathematics Program (Muncie, Indiana).
7. Boston College Series (Grades 8–12).

BIOLOGICAL SCIENCES

1. Biological Sciences Curriculum Study (directed by Dr. Grobman for the American Institute of Biological Sciences).

PHYSICAL SCIENCE

1. Physical Science Study Committee (with headquarters at Massachusetts Institute of Technology).
2. Chemical Education Materials Study (carried on under the

American Chemical Society by Dr. Arthur Campbell at Harvey Mudd College, Claremont, California).

    3. The Chemical Bond Group (Earlham College).

There have also been efforts in many local secondary schools to bring up to date the content of courses in physics, chemistry, mathematics, social studies, as well as in other fields. The recommended materials for courses in mathematics have, nevertheless, been severely criticized by several college professors of mathematics as being suitable only for the more capable students. It seems quite likely that the use of most of the new mathematics curriculum materials will be confined to special sections of superior students.

English. There has also been increased attention in recent years to the improvement of reading. Most schools now have required remedial courses for poor readers and elective courses for all who wish to increase their reading speed and comprehension.

Spurred on by criticisms from various educators and a recommendation by Dr. Conant, increased attention is being given to training in clear and correct English, both oral and written.

Modern foreign language. The need for bringing up-to-date the contents of secondary school courses is not confined to the fields of science and mathematics. Indeed, the content of foreign languages—even Latin—is currently shifting. In modern languages, the content is now being selected with the view to developing a knowledge and appreciation of the culture, and an ability to converse rather than upon learning to read and translate.

History and social studies. The content of courses in history and social studies (see p. 22) is undergoing rapid change. Much more attention is being given to the cultures and peoples of Latin America, Asia and Africa, and instruction is being related to the controversial political and economic problems of the day.

More and more schools are including instruction about the nature of Communism.[3] Both the National Education Association and the American Legion have recommended that such a course be required in all schools.

---

[3] See "A Selected Annotated Bibliography to Assist Teachers in Teaching About Communism," by Merrill F. Hartshorn and T. Marcus Gillespie (Washington, D.C.: National Council for Social Studies, 1961).

Listening. Increased attention is also being given to training students in effective listening—increasing their ability to understand and analyze what is heard and to recognize propaganda.

Sex education and health education. Many schools have abandoned special courses in sex education in recent years in favor of treating some phases of sex education in courses on health, science, and in physical education. There has also been a trend to give somewhat more attention to health education in courses in science and physical education.

Vocational course. Because the nature of occupations in which present secondary school students will engage will undoubtedly change, there is a widespread demand for reexamination of the secondary school vocational program. Some courses in vocational education have been modified so that they will be better coordinated with activities performed on the job and with on-the-spot vocational training conducted by employers.

Training in study procedures. Because many more students plan to go to college, because of the increased use of lectures in high school, and because of the increased attention to the underachiever and the drop-out, many schools are devoting attention to training students to take notes. Increased attention is also being given to training students to use reference books, periodicals and newspapers, to prepare papers and to study for examinations.

BIBLIOGRAPHY

Ahrendt, M. H., *The Revolution in Mathematics,* National Council of Teachers of Mathematics. Washington, D.C.: National Education Association, 1960, 90 pp.

Brickell, Henry M., *et al., Commissioner's 1961 Catalogue of Educational Change.* Albany, N.Y.: State Education Department, 1962, 200 pp. Description of changes in schools in New York.

Frasier, Alexander, and Harold Wagren, *Guidelines for Television.* Washington, D.C.: National Education Association, 1960, 80 pp.

Gross, R. E., "Emerging Horizons for the Social Studies," *Social Education,* Vol. 24 (January, 1960), pp. 21–4.

Halvety, Julius H., *et al., Mathematics for the Academically Talented Student.* Washington, D.C.: National Education Association and National Council of Teachers of Mathematics, 1959, 48 pp.

Harris, Paul E., Marshall Schmitt, and Albert L. Petty, *Industrial Arts: An Analysis of 39 State Curriculum Guides*. Washington, D.C.: U.S. Office of Education, 1960, 76 pp.

Hartshorn, Merrill R., "Current Critical Issue in Secondary Education— Social Studies in the Comprehensive Secondary School," *Bulletin of the N.A.S.S.P.*, No. 254 (April, 1961), pp. 312–26.

Hull, Richard B., *The Uses of Television in Education*. Chicago: North Central Association of Colleges and Secondary Schools, 1961, 32 pp.

McKibben, Margaret J., "New Developments in Secondary-School Science," *The Education Digest*, Vol. XXVI, No. 7 (March, 1961), pp. 34–8.

McLure, W. P., "The Future of Vocational and Technical Education," *Bulletin of the N.A.S.S.P.*, No. 262 (February, 1961), pp. 7–12.

National Education Association, *Mathematics for the Academically Talented Student in the Secondary School* (1959), 48 pp.; *Modern Foreign Language and the Academically Talented Student* (1960), 96 pp.; *Science for the Academically Talented Student in the Secondary School* (1959), 64 pp.

Otto, Arleen C., *New Designs in Homemaking Programs in Junior High Schools*. New York: Bureau of Publications, Teachers College, Columbia University, 1958, xii + 100 pp.

Planning for Excellence in High School Science. National Science Teachers Association of the National Education Association, 1961, 67 pp.

Quest for Quality. Washington, D.C.: National School Boards Association, and American Association of School Administrators, 1960. A series of 48-page booklets describing superior practices in each of a number of schools in the United States.

Renner, John W. (Science), Kenneth E. Brown (Mathematics), Marjorie C. Johnston (Foreign Languages), Arno Jewett (English Language Arts), "Keeping Up-to-date With Developments in Science, Mathematics, Modern Foreign Languages and English Language Arts," *Bulletin of the N.A.S.S.P.*, No. 254 (April, 1961), pp. 248–54.

Rinker, Floyd, Walter Auffenberg, Galen Jones, John E. Dobbin. "New Developments in Secondary School Programs and Services," *Bulletin of the N.A.S.S.P.*, No. 254 (April, 1961), pp. 189–95.

Rosskop, Myron S., *et al.*, "New Developments in Secondary-School Mathematics," *Bulletin of the N.A.S.S.P.*, No. 247 (May, 1959), 288 pp.

Schulz, Richard W., "Quality Science for the Senior High School," *Bulletin of the N.A.S.S.P.*, No. 260 (December, 1960), p. 77.

"The Changing Business Program in High School," *Business Education Forum*. *The Education Digest*, Vol. XXVI, No. 8 (April, 1961), pp. 47–50.

CHAPTER V

Class Organization and Management

Independent and Group Learning

Greater provision for independent study. Prior to the last quarter century, most secondary schools expected students to spend from 40 to 60 minutes in preparation for each daily class meeting of some 40 to 45 minutes. Beginning about 1930 was the trend toward longer class periods in part of which the learner studied or prepared his new lesson, aided and supervised by the teacher. This trend, along with the development of clubs and other extracurricular activities and the practice of permitting students to take a larger number of subjects, has resulted in the great decrease in the use of study halls. Unfortunately along with this trend there has been until very recently a decline in the average amount of time spent in the library, in home study, and in other types of independent study.

In recent years there has been a demand by educators and the public for more independent study by the students. This demand together with the increase in the proportion of young people going to college where skills and habits in independent study are so important has resulted in increased requirements for home study. The Trump Plan of team teaching (see Chapter VI) calls for a considerable amount of independent study. More and more schools are providing laboratories with individual small carrels equipped with tape recorders for independent study as well as for group instruction in foreign languages.

Planning Learning Activities

Relationship to objectives in education. Teachers and those engaged in course-of-study construction are beginning to plan learning activities around more definite objectives—objectives of secondary education, of the particular subject, and of each unit of the subject. More teachers are planning learning activities which they

37

think will result in the development of desirable, intellectual, social, and physical skills, habits, and attitudes, as well as the acquisition of information which will contribute to effectiveness in home living, earning a living, leisure activities, and community life.

Learner participation in planning activities. Although perhaps fewer teachers today are permitting students to play a major part in planning their learning activities, there has been a steady trend toward using the suggestions of the individual student and the group in planning some aspects of the learning activities.

Homework. Stimulated by suggestions from parents and educators, there has been since about 1955 a trend toward requiring more homework. This trend has been accelerated by the spreading belief that the subject achievement of secondary school students should be increased.

Much of the homework, however, tends to be of a slightly different type—especially in the junior high school. Homework now involves more study and practice and less preparation of written work (which may have been "supervised" by parents or friends and which required time-consuming checking by the teacher).

Use of Library Materials

With the decreased use of study halls, there has been much less opportunity for students to use library materials and for teachers to give assignments involving study in the library. To some extent this condition has been ameliorated by establishing in classrooms small collections of books appropriate for the courses taught there.

In recent years there has been a slight but definitely noticeable reverse trend toward providing more free periods (this is partly a result of a longer school day). Because more students are going to college, there is increased emphasis upon preparation for college, so that greater opportunities for use of library and library materials are being provided in most schools. By 1962 more than 80 per cent of all secondary schools had libraries operating at least through the school day and there were approximately 15,000 trained librarians in secondary schools. About half of these librarians were in large schools—only a very small percentage of schools with less than 250 students employ full-time trained librarians.

Discussion as a Learning Activity

A pronounced trend in classroom procedure is the greater use of discussion, including the discussion of controversial issues. Not only does discussion develop greater interest in a topic but—if properly managed—it also helps to develop the pupils' skills in reasoning, in analyzing spoken materials, in careful listening, and in understanding the speech of others.

Types of organization for discussion. Increasing use has been made of the panel discussion in which each of the members of a small group is responsible for presenting a small part of the topic and participates in discussion on the material presented. Cooperative planning of learner activities and evaluation of news and its sources are used widely.

A practice which has been in existence for several decades is the division of the class into several groups, each of which makes an intensive study of several aspects of the topic and discusses not only procedures but the topic itself.

A relatively small number of secondary school teachers have made use of socio-drama and rôle-playing for presenting materials to the class for discussion.

Controversial issues. Since the decline of McCarthyism increasing attention has been given to the matter of discussing controversial issues in the classroom and to the necessity for providing definite training in the evaluation of propaganda.

In 1961, the National Education Association prepared and published a bulletin on controversial issues in the classroom.[1] It set forth a number of classroom hints for teachers and administrators, a description of current practices and policies at Des Moines, Denver, Tampa, Champaign, Jackson, and Evanston, and the policies of the New Jersey State Board of Education and the Commission on Education Policy of the California Teachers Association.

Student Citizenship and Discipline

The increases in knowledge of human relations and of the effects of punishment and positive approaches toward the motivation of

---

[1] Earl H. Hanson and Myrtle M. Bonn, Co-chairmen. *Controversial Issues in the Classroom* (Washington, D.C.: National Education Association, 1961), 30 pp.

students as well as the rise in juvenile crime and delinquency have focused attention on student discipline and citizenship.

Shifts in basic ideas. A shift in attitudes toward discipline has grown out of a better knowledge of the effects of discipline upon young people. Although punishment may relieve the teacher and deter potential evil-doers to some degree, it has caused a considerable number of young people to develop very unfortunate attitudes toward school, adult authority, and adult standards in general. Many of the young people who have dropped out of school have indicated that one of the principal reasons was disciplinary treatment. Educators who have studied the histories of youthful criminals in correctional institutions also believe that the development of socially unacceptable attitudes is frequently attributable to school and its disciplinary program.

For the last several decades there has been a trend toward emphasizing the development of self-governing habits within young people rather than relying on the use of punishment to compel desirable behavior. There has been for some time an increasing tendency on the part of teachers to attempt to develop civic pride on the part of the individual student and to give youngsters constructive and interesting things to do as a means of developing cooperation with the program and activities of the school.

Student participation. Students have been permitted and encouraged to participate in the government and the management of certain aspects of school life which are of great concern to them. For a time there was a trend toward setting up student governments with elected student judges and courts somewhat after the fashion of the famous George Junior Republic of a half century ago. These experiments have usually been unsuccessful and a reverse trend can now be observed.

A steadily increasing number of schools are employing another type of student participation in management and government—through some representative body such as the student council. The student council not only formulates and presents to students and faculty student attitudes and opinions concerning student behavior, but it is also responsible for management in fields in which students most commonly participate—the management of clubs, assemblies, noon-hour patrols, library, cafeteria, and driving and parking of student automobiles.

In recent years, an increasing portion of the public has come to believe in—and in many instances to insist upon—greater use of punishment by teachers. At the junior high school level at least corporal punishment is being used to a slightly greater extent than in the previous few decades. A recent trend is toward more encouragement of more exercise on the part of students as a means of relieving their tensions and thereby reducing the problem of discipline.

Guidance and discipline. There has also been a shift away from the idea that counselors should be rarely if ever employed in connection with matters of discipline. Counselors are used to make a case study of chronic or serious offenders with a view to counselling the youngster and conferring with parents, and advising the principal and the teacher of relevant facts concerning the misbehaving individual and the probable effects of various approaches to the problem.

BIBLIOGRAPHY

Anderson, Stuart A., "Where Students Maintain Much of Their Own Discipline," *The Nation's Schools,* Vol. 67, No. 5 (May, 1961), pp. 70–74, 168–70.

Asubel, David P., "A New Look at Classroom Discipline," *The Phi Delta Kappan,* Vol. 43, No. 1 (October, 1961), pp. 25–30.

Chamberlain, Robert J., "The Role of the Principal in Discipline," *Bulletin of the N.A.S.S.P.,* No. 248 (September, 1959), pp. 139–43.

Discipline and Delinquency. A symposium in *Phi Delta Kappan,* Vol. XLI, No. 3 (December, 1959).

Gulley, Halbert E., *Discussion Conference and Group Process.* New York: Holt, Rinehart, & Winston, 1960, 320 pp.

Hock, Louise E., *Using Committees in the Classroom.* New York: Holt, Rinehart, & Winston, 1958, 55 pp.

Jensen, Gale E., *et al.,* "The Dynamics of Instructional Groups," *Fifty-ninth Yearbook* of the National Society for the Study of Education (1960), 286 pp. See especially Chapter III, "The Role of the Teacher."

Mills, H. H., and Harl R. Douglass, *Teaching in High School.* New York: Ronald Press, 1957, Chapters 9–12.

Mueller, Theodore, "New Trends in Modern Foreign Language Teachings," *The Education Digest,* Vol. XXV, No. 8 (April, 1960), p. 49.

National Education Association. *Controversial Issues in the Classroom* (1961), 50 pp.

Parody, Ovid F., *The High School Principal and Staff Deal with Discipline.* New York: Bureau of Publication, Teachers College, Columbia University, 1958, 90 pp.

Stack, Edward M., *The Language Laboratory and Modern Language Teaching.* New York: Oxford University Press, 1960, 148 pp.

Studies of the Utilization of Staff, Buildings, and Audio-Visual Aids. Washington, D.C.: Office of Education, Department of Health, Education and Welfare, 1959.

"Ten Years of Educational Television: The Uses of Television in Education," *The Education Digest,* Vol. XXVII, No. 1 (September, 1961), pp. 28–31.

Wellington, C. B., and Jean Wellington, *Teaching for Critical Thinking.* New York: McGraw-Hill Book Company, 1961.

What Policies Should Guide the Handling of Controversial Issues? Washington, D.C.: National Education Association, 1959.

CHAPTER VI

Team Teaching, Teaching Machines, and Programmed Learning

The Nature of Team Teaching

In recent years, team teaching—two or more teachers operating as a team in planning and giving instruction to groups of learners—has taken a variety of forms. Although already begun in some secondary schools the team teaching idea was accelerated greatly by activities of the Commission on Staff Utilization of the National Association of Secondary-School Principals, the availability of grants from national educational foundations, and the results of numerous experiments conducted over a period of years and reported in the successive January issues of *The Bulletin of the National Association of Secondary-School Principals* beginning in 1958. The best known and most commonly used plan is the Trump Plan of team teaching, so named because Professor Lloyd Trump, Associate Secretary of the National Association of Secondary-School Principals, was the consultant for the Commission on Staff Utilization and presented to them a plan which was adopted by the Commission and publicized greatly by the *Bulletin*. The principle features of the Trump Plan are:

1. Groups of students (from 50 to 200, but usually 100 to 125) meet to hear lectures for which the speaker was allowed adequate time on his teaching load. Trump recommended that approximately 40 per cent of the student's time on a given subject be spent at such lectures.
2. Discussions are carried on in smaller groups (12 to 15 students). These discussion groups could be led by any of the instructors of the class or even, in some instances, by teachers' aides. It was recommended that approximately 20 per cent of the time devoted to a particular subject be spent in such discussion groups.
3. Students—individually or in very small groups—are to pursue a course of independent study in laboratories, libraries, study

carrels, or study halls. Approximately 40 per cent of the time spent on any given subject was to be spent on such independent study.

4. Teachers are to be relieved of time-consuming routine tasks by assistants (to read papers and to prepare and score examinations, to assist in supervision of halls, playgrounds, and similar places) and typists and clerks (to help with mimeographing and other clerical work).

Use of features of the Trump Plan. For a number of years the consensus has been that more use should be made of carefully prepared and properly illustrated lectures to large groups by selected lecturers; greater use is already being made of group discussion in class periods. Also there has been a definite swing toward greater use of independent study, not only as a method of developing quality education in the secondary schools but also as a preparation for college.

Opposition to the Trump Plan. Although many educators believe that at least some form of team teaching should be employed in many classes in secondary school, the plan has met considerable opposition. This opposition is based on the feeling that the plan decreases the amount of valuable pupil-teacher personal relationships and counselling and tends to emphasize unduly the acquisition of information. Also, it is difficult to provide adequately for independent study or indeed to motivate all students so as to prevent problems of discipline. Another difficulty is in the invidious comparisons involved in selecting the chairman or the lecturer for the large groups—the same sort of phenomenon that has slowed down the spread of merit rating and merit salary increases.

The lack of a sufficient number of large rooms for group lectures and small rooms for discussion groups is not an insuperable difficulty; the size of a classroom may be altered, especially in new buildings planned for flexibility.

Reported results obtained from the use of team teaching seem rather favorable, although in a number of instances the experimental situation was a modification of the Trump Plan.

Machine Teaching and the Use of
Programmed Course-of-Study Materials

The belief that students should be permitted to proceed at their individual pace and the tendency toward "technology" has given rise to the use of teaching machines. Since 1955, more than a hundred of these have been marketed at prices ranging from about ten dollars to more than two thousand.

Types of teaching machines. A large variety of teaching machines has been put on the market. These machines usually fall into one of two categories: those which present the student with a number of alternative possibilities from which he selects a correct response, and those which present the student with blanks in which he is expected to fill in the correct response. Both types present the learner with the sequential items in a given course of study in logical order following a definite program. "Write-in" machines, computers, punch board machines, "scramble book" machines, automatic ratio machines, and programmed textbooks are now available.

Basic ideas of machine teaching. The principal characteristics of machine teaching are:

1. Programmed learning materials arranged in adequate sequential order are employed.
2. Mechanical devices for testing the mastery of a certain idea or bit of information are employed.
3. The individual student may proceed to master materials at his own rate.
4. The teacher is relieved of certain teaching and testing activities.
5. The learner is prevented from "cheating": he cannot look ahead to answers.
6. The student can correct mistakes before proceeding further.
7. The student is encouraged by a prompt report on his performance.

Opposition to use of machines. Many—perhaps most—teachers are not convinced of the effectiveness of teaching machines.

The use of teaching machines has very serious limitations. The principal drawback is that this type of instruction constitutes a means for outside control of the curriculum. Also, it emphasizes the acquisition of factual subject matter at the expense of the development of intellectual skills and desirable ideals, attitudes, interests, and tastes. Since the general trend is away from acquisition of factual material as an objective of education, the prospects for widespread adoption of teaching machines within the next few years is not an inviting one in spite of the aggressive campaign being waged by their proponents and manufacturers.

Programmed course-of-study materials. Any type of teaching machine is based on a sequential course of materials, usually referred to as programmed course-of-study materials. Indeed the effectiveness of the machines as educational instruments depends very largely upon these programmed materials, and a considerable number of teachers and administrators are refraining from the use of machines until better programmed material has been developed.

Usually the programmed course of study is the "scrambled book" type. For example, in *English 2600* (published by Harcourt, Brace, and World Book Company in 1960), there appears in the first paragraph on page 1 the incomplete sentence, "Fred tore ———— ————." The next sentence points out that the first sentence is incomplete and needs an object. Two pages later the student finds a paragraph which explains that *shirt* is the object and that the sentence is now complete as "Fred tore his shirt." To the question then posed: "Which word receives the action of the verb *tore?*" the student is supposed to write in *shirt*.

Many educators are not convinced that the programmed materials which have been developed to date—even when used together with teaching machines—are as effective as a teacher with a good textbook. They also question the desirability of having students work along individually without explanation or encouragement and without the personal contact with the instructor. Also programmed textbooks make it possible for the student to cheat.

Furthermore, uniform programmed course-of-study materials do not make adequate provision for differences in individual ability, since they emphasize the rate at which the student proceeds rather than permitting the presentation of materials to be adapted to the abilities, interests, and potentialities of the individual student.

Although the results of a number of experiments seem to indicate a slight superiority of the results obtained by the use of teaching machines, and programmed materials, the critics point out that many of the experiments have been conducted under unusually good conditions. The inference is that similar results could not be gotten generally. The critics also argue that many of the available outcomes of education—such as analytical thinking, problem solving, group skills in cooperative work, and so on—are not well provided for teaching by machines or the use of programmed textbooks. Many object to the surrender of control of courses of study to the authors of programmed materials. Others point out that with the use of expensive programmed materials, experimentation and continuous course-of-study improvement would be difficult.

BIBLIOGRAPHY

Andrews, Robert G., "How to Improve Instruction with Teaching Teams," *School Management*, Vol. 4, No. 11 (November, 1960), pp. 50–5, 116. Description and evaluation at Park Forest, Illinois High School.

Lobb, M. D., M. F. Noall, H. L. Slechenmyer, "What Are Some Promising Practices in Team Teaching? *The Bulletin of the N.A.S.S.P.*, No. 255 (April, 1960), pp. 2–7.

Lund, Kenneth W., "It's Time for a Breakthrough," *The Education Digest*, Vol. XXV, No. 4 (December, 1959), p. 18.

Morse, Arthur D., *Schools of Tomorrow*. New York: Doubleday and Company, Inc., 1960, 191 pp. A report on experiments with team teaching, guidance of bright children, television.

Porter, D. A., "A Critical Review of a Portion of the Literature on Teaching Devices," *Harvard Education Review*, Vol. 26 (Spring, 1957), pp. 126–47.

"Self-Instruction Devices," *Audio-Visual Instruction* (April, 1961). Articles on teaching machines and "scrambled books"; glossary of teaching machine terms, name and addresses of manufacturers with brief descriptions of their products.

Trump, J. Lloyd, *Images of the Future; A New Approach to the Secondary School*. Urbana, Ill.: Commission on the Experimental Study of the Utilization of the Staff in the Secondary School, 1959, 48 pp.

———, *New Horizons for Secondary School Teachers*. Urbana, Ill.: Commission on the Experimental Study of the Utilization of the Staff in the Secondary School, 1957, 35 pp.

Team Teaching, Tapes and Large Class. Reports on Staff Utilization. The January issues of *The Bulletin of the N.A.S.S.P.*, 1958, 1959, 1960, 1961, and 1962. Reports on experiments with team teaching, tape recordings, and teaching large classes.

Weiss, T. M., "Critique of the Team Approach," *Education Forum*, Vol. 24 (January, 1960), pp. 207–8.

"What Is Happening in the Use of Technology in the Classroom and in Class Size—Report of a Survey," *The Bulletin of the N.A.S.S.P.*, No. 264 (April, 1961), pp. 328–30.

Wittich, Walter A., "Teaching Machines, Practical and Probable," *The Nation's Schools*, Vol. 66, No. 2 (August, 1960), pp. 64–5, 84–90.

CHAPTER VII

Adapting Instruction
to the Individual

One of the outstanding educational trends in recent years has been that of attempts to adapt instruction to the individual. There had long been attempts to make provision for boys and girls of greater ability and for boys and girls of lesser ability.

Plans for More Capable Students

Advanced courses. In recent years a number of plans for adapting instruction to more capable students have been developed. Prominent among these has been ability or homogeneous grouping, honors courses and "advanced placement" courses in a number of subjects in which students study materials ordinarily encountered in first year college courses and as a result might either obtain college credit or at least be placed in more advanced sections in this subject when admitted to college.[1] The New York State Education Department has prepared a series of syllabi in various fields designed to encourage high schools to offer academically superior pupils instruction of a caliber that may indeed warrant advanced placement or credit upon college entrance. Honors courses and other special courses, including seminars, have been developed in an increasing number of secondary schools. In these courses the students study more difficult and advanced materials than those presented to the average student.

The development of these advanced courses has slowed down because, in some cases, the college credit expected by the secondary administrators has not been given. High school principals are now gathering more precise information as to which colleges will give

---

[1] At Yale University, for example, entering freshmen are assigned on the basis of tests and previous grades to the appropriate one of three successive semesters of mathematics study.

credit for advanced placement courses and are using this information to advise students about enrollment in such courses.

A number of schools, stimulated by popular demand, are using grouping techniques and making other special provisions for the abler students not only in academic fields but also in art, music, shopwork, household arts, and physical education.

Adapting to the creative student. Much more attention is being given to students who possess what have come to be called "creative abilities and impulses." In the departments of psychology of the University of Minnesota, the University of Chicago, and at the University of Utah, techniques have been developed for identifying the "creative" child. In a small but increasing number of secondary schools, these or similar techniques have been employed and learning activities and materials have been devised to satisfy creative impulses and to avoid the unfortunate personality development which grow out of frustration.

Acceleration of the more able. More and more secondary schools are making provision for bright students to gain a year. Such students have been permitted to carry a larger number of subjects which—together with attendance in summer school—has enabled them to complete their requirements in a year earlier. Indeed, in a few schools it has become possible—as recommended by Dr. Conant in his *The American High School*—to complete six years of secondary education in four years.[2]

Although this trend has met with very firm opposition, it continues to spread and, in view of the many years now required to complete medical or legal studies, graduate work, or specialized work in scientific, technological and industrial fields, this trend is not likely to be reversed.

Earlier groupings were based primarily on the so-called intelligence tests and on previous subject grades. Now other factors—such as teachers' estimates of student drive, industry and special interest inventories, aptitude tests, and home environment data—are also taken into consideration.

The effectiveness of instruction in classes formed for abler stu-

---

[2] Recommended also by Dr. Sam M. Lambert, Director of Research Division of the National Education Association in a speech to the Fourth National School for Teachers' Salary Schedules.

dents has been conditioned by the degree to which the teacher has employed appropriate learning materials and methods. In more and more schools, sections for the bright student or for the less able student are being assigned only to teachers who have had special preparation.

Plans for the Less Promising, the Handicapped, and the "Under-Achievers"

The increase in the number of students entering the senior high school has emphasized the need for special provision for the student of lesser ability. The problem is not solved by the elective system or by enrolling such students in vocational subjects.

Special sections. It has become clear that in order to play his part in the world today, the less able student must have an adequate general background in science, mathematics, history and the social studies, English, and physical and health education. In the majority of junior high schools, and in an increasing number of senior high schools and four-year high schools, special sections in various subjects are being formed in which specially trained teachers provide the instruction most suitable to the interests, the learning capacities, and the more probable needs of the less able student.

It became increasingly evident in the 1930's and 1940's that the practice of automatic annual promotion in the elementary school was contributing to the problem of instructing the less able students in the junior high school—particularly in the fields of reading and other language arts, and arithmetic. Many junior high schools are compelled to provide remedial sections for those youngsters who would not profit best by attempting to do the conventional work in the seventh-grade subjects.

According to reports by the Research Division of the National Education Association, in 1960–1961 nearly two-thirds of school districts of more than 2,500 people made some provision for remedial instruction. In an increasing number of schools these sections are continued through the eighth grade and even—though to a lesser extent—through the ninth grade.

Special curricula. In some schools, as at Alhambra and Fresno, California, High School, a special curriculum has been developed for the least able students. Through the eleventh grade these students are taught academic subjects in special sections with especially prepared teachers. In a considerable number of high schools, an effort is being made to meet the problem by having students of various academic abilities and interests register in different curricula requiring different amounts of academic ability and interest.

Failure, retardation, and withdrawal from school. The general tightening up of educational standards has halted the trend away from giving failing grades to secondary school students. Indeed, there is a slight trend toward giving failing grades to those students who make little effort to achieve their full potential and consequently learn very little.

Not only are fewer students dropping out before completing the twelfth grade,[3] but attempts are being made to reduce the number of dropouts, particularly of those students of average or better academic ability. More attention is being given to the expense of participating in social and other types of student activities, to social discrimination against students of lower socioeconomic levels, as well as to the phases of the curriculum and the methods of teaching which are not effective to the type of student who constitutes a large proportion of those who drop out.

For several decades there have been attempts to decrease the number of students dropping out of school before completing senior high school. Much more attention has been given to the problem in recent years as it has become increasingly difficult for such young people to obtain employment and as the increased incidence of juvenile delinquency among drop-outs has come to the attention of educational and civil authorities. In 1961 a $190,000 grant from The Ford Foundation enabled the National Education Association to institute a careful study of the drop-outs with a view to developing recommendations for more effective education in secondary schools. The problem not only involves adaptation of instruction, but also counselling for participation in social and other extracurricular activities. Many are coming to believe, with Dr. Lambert,

---

[3] Of 1,000 pupils in the fifth grade in 1950–1951, 885 entered the ninth grade in the fall of 1954, 586 graduated, and 308 entered college in the fall of 1960. *N.E.A. Research Bulletin* No. 39 (February 1961), p. 27.

that a really adequate program of guidance through the twelfth grade might reduce by half the present number of drop-outs.

Special approaches to students from slum areas. Dr. J. B. Conant, who has been engaged for a number of years in the study of various problems of secondary education, has declared that social dynamite is accumulating in the slums[4] of big cities and threatens to explode there unless education is overhauled. He says that the responsibility of secondary schools in large cities should be extended to provide job and educational counselling of all youths under twenty-one whether they are in school or not. Dr. Robert Havighurst of the University of Chicago and Dean Lindley Stiles of the University of Wisconsin had previously pointed out that rather a large section of our population lives in areas of substandard culture and economic opportunity. The children in such areas have a less than average chance of completing high school and many of them become serious behavior problems. Professor Havighurst advocated the establishment of a special school for those in this latter group (which he calls "unadaptives") who are still of school age.

In Detroit[5] there has been carried on an experiment of establishing closer contact between the schools and parents in substandard communities. This approach seems to improve the attitude of both the students and the parents toward school, to improve the school work of a great many of the students, and to reduce juvenile delinquency.

The Ford Foundation in 1961 also announced grants for programs calculated to help school children in slum neighborhoods of Detroit, Philadelphia, St. Louis, and Richmond, California, bringing to a total of more than three million dollars the amount of Ford Foundation grants for programs to improve education in blighted neighborhoods of the nation's large cities.

Closely related is the trend to give more attention to migrant children—children of parents who move about following employment opportunities in the harvesting of crops. These children come largely from families of low income and cultural background and

---

[4] James B. Conant, *Slums and Suburbs* (McGraw-Hill Book Co., 1961).

[5] *Increasing the Competence of Culturally Different Pupils by Improving Teaching and Community Service,* Detroit Public Schools, Mimeographed (February 5, 1960).

homes and are in large part recent immigrants. Much legislation has been passed providing for better living conditions and education for these people.

Plans for the under-achievers. Under-achievers include students of all degrees of learning capacity—bright students doing only average work, average students doing inferior work, and poor students doing less well than possible for them. More attention is being focused on the under-achiever and attempts are being made to discover the reasons for his failure to realize his full potential.

Some success along these lines has been achieved as the result of the increased number of counselors and the improved quality of their preparation. Conferences with parents of under-achievers are held not with the view of having them assist in stimulating the student to better work (in many instances such stimulation does more harm than good), but to obtain information from them about the student and his plans, interests, attitudes, and activities, and to enlist their cooperation in the rehabilitation of the under-achiever.

Promotions and types of diplomas. A number of laymen have criticized the trend toward keeping to a minimum the number of students receiving failing grades. Most educators maintain that failing a youngster in a required course serves no purpose, that the student usually does as poorly in the repetition of the course, and that much harm is done to his attitudes toward himself, the school, learning, and adult authority in general. There has, however, been a slight increase in the proportion of failures given in elective subjects.

There has also been much discussion of the advisability of giving different kinds of diplomas on the basis of the different courses followed and grades achieved. This trend suffered a severe setback when Dr. J. B. Conant recommended instead that a uniform diploma be used with a record on the back of subjects taken and the student's achievement, as well as other pertinent facts.

Identification of Deviates and Appropriate Adaptation of Instruction

Ability groupings in recent years tend more and more to be based on measures of academic ability such as the intelligence quotient and mental age, but also on teachers' estimates of the student's drive, character, and temperament, and the functional and social level of the home and family. There is a growing tendency to assume that children of relatively uneducated parents or children who come from homes with little in the way of good books and magazines, and especially children who come from bilingual homes, probably have more academic potential than the scores on intelligence tests would indicate. Decisions about the probable academic achievement of high school students are coming to be based on clinical approaches and on the counselors' recommendations. Also used are the results of interest questionnaires and the testimony of teachers and parents as to the interests of the youngster.

Emotionally disturbed students. There is an increased incidence of emotional disturbances among high school students. This constitutes a problem not only to the teachers and school authorities but to the parents and to the young people themselves. A larger proportion of these youngsters are being identified. As the number of counselors increases and the quality of their training improves, more and more of these students are referred to the school psychologist and recommended for psychiatric treatment. A considerable number of schools now have access to the services of a school psychologist, and a small but increasing number have access to psychiatric services as well.

Special education. Increasing numbers of boys and girls who are handicapped—whether mentally, emotionally, or physically—are completing their secondary education. Many states have set up special funds for the teaching of classes for the handicapped and for the training of teachers for the handicapped. As a result there have been added to the program of an increasing number of secondary schools provisions for teaching the very dull, those who have severely impaired eyesight and hearing, for cripples, spastics and other types of handicapped children.

The number of schools giving some sort of speech therapy for stutterers, lispers, and those with other speech defects has increased until in 1960–1961 at least two-thirds of the urban districts were so doing. Teachers are also being given some in-service training by speech specialists in the techniques of working with young people with speech defects. This training emphasizes the psychological practices involved.

BIBLIOGRAPHY

Administrative Procedures and School Practices for the Academically Talented Student in the Secondary School. Washington, D.C.: N.A.S.S.P., 1960, 224 pp.

Anderson, Kenneth, *Research on the Academically Talented.* Washington, D.C.: The National Education Association, 1961.

Anderson, Lester W., J. E. Fergason, Stewart B. Atkinson, "How to Modify the Curriculum to Benefit the Academically Talented Student," *The Bulletin of the N.A.S.S.P.,* No. 264 (April, 1961), pp. 243–47.

Bish, Charles E., and Minnis Gilliland, "A Program for the Academically Talented in Science," *The Bulletin of the N.A.S.S.P.,* No. 260 (December, 1960), pp. 138–44.

Chaffee, Everett, "Programs for the Gifted in California Secondary Schools," *The Bulletin of the N.A.S.S.P.,* No. 253 (March, 1960), pp. 110–14.

Conant, James B., *Slums and Suburbs.* New York: McGraw-Hill Book Co., 1961.

Condon, John J., Elsie F. Gibbs, and O. Meredith Parry, "How Can Summer Schools Enrich and Accelerate the Educational Programs of Capable Students?" *The Bulletin of the N.A.S.S.P.,* No. 255 (April, 1960), pp. 121–27.

Cuony, E. R., "Integration for Educable Mentally Retarded Pupils in the Junior High School," *The Bulletin of the N.A.S.S.P.,* No. 259 (November, 1960), pp. 87–90.

Davis, L. R., and Jacqueline Davis, "What Principals Should Know About Remedial Reading," *The Clearing House,* Vol. 29 (January, 1955), pp. 298–300.

Dudley, D. A., *et al.,* "Advanced Placement Programs in Secondary Schools," *The Bulletin of the N.A.S.S.P.,* No. 242 (December, 1958), pp. 1–183. Contains descriptions of programs in a number of high schools and a syllabus for eleven different subjects.

Ferguson, W. J., "A Report on a Junior High School Program for the Gifted," *The Bulletin of the N.A.S.S.P.,* No. 259 (November, 1960), pp. 79–87.

Harnly, Paul W., and Harry D. Lovelass, "How Have Summer Schools Been Used to Enrich the Educational Program for the Academically Talented?" *The Bulletin of the N.A.S.S.P.,* No. 246 (May, 1959), pp. 182–86.

Havighurst, Robert J., "Metropolitan Development and the Educational System," *The School Review,* Vol. 69 (Autumn, 1961), pp. 251–68. The underprivileged as a serious socioeducational problem.

Hogenmiller, Robert E., "A Science and Mathematics Curriculum for Terminal Students in High School," *The Bulletin of the N.A.S.S.P.,* No. 240 (October, 1958), pp. 109–17.

Langworthy, Stanley, *et al., The Slow Learner in Secondary School.* Trenton, New Jersey: Secondary School Teachers Association, 1961 Yearbook.

Miller, Leonard M., *et al., Guidance for the Underachiever with Superior Ability.* U.S. Office of Education Bulletin No. 25 (1961), 86 pp.

National Education Association, *Program Provisions for the Mathematically Gifted Student in the Secondary School,* 1957, 32 pp.

Newton, D. E., "Curricular and Instructional Practices for Superior Students," *The Bulletin of the N.A.S.S.P.,* Vol. 45, No. 262 (February, 1961), pp. 23–7.

Paschal, Elizabeth, *Encouraging the Excellent: Special Programs for Gifted and Talented Students.* New York: The Fund for the Advancement of Education, 1960, 79 pp.

Rossier, Charles Pope, "Teaching English to Gifted Students," *The Clearing House,* Vol. 33 (March, 1959), pp. 415–18.

Salario, Morris, "The Mentally Handicapped Child in High School," *The Education Digest,* Vol. XXVI, No. 1 (September, 1960), pp. 45–7.

Silverman, Hirsch Lazaar, "Educational 'Unadaptives' and the Schools," *The Bulletin of the N.A.S.S.P.,* No. 240 (October, 1958), pp. 129–33.

"The Academically Talented," *School and Society,* Vol. 87 (April 11, 1959). Entire issue, several articles.

Torrence, Paul E., "Problems of Highly Creative Children," *Gifted Child Quarterly,* 5 (Summer, 1961), pp. 31–4. Summarized in *Education Digest,* 27–3 (November, 1961), pp. 40–2.

——, *Talent and Education.* Minneapolis: University of Minnesota Press, 1960, 210 pp.

Yorgan, D. G., "Lincoln Junior High School Administers an Accelerated Program for Superior Students," *The Bulletin of the N.A.S.S.P.,* No. 254 (March, 1960), pp. 65–70.

CHAPTER VIII

Evaluating and Reporting
Learner Status and Growth

Adaptation of Evaluation
to the Objectives of Education

From about 1910 to 1940 the educational status and progress of students in various school subjects was evaluated by objective written tests and final examinations emphasizing the factual knowledge. In recent decades there has been a trend toward basing such evaluation on data relative to the status and growth of students in broader fields—including, for example, the measures of intellectual skills, attitudes toward and interests in social issues, other people, social institutions, mores, and themselves. This has been part of the movement to develop programs and methods of evaluation which would measure status and growth toward the achievement of the avowed objectives of education. On the other hand, the increasing use of teaching machines, programmed learning materials, and the lecture method has reversed this trend, though only slightly as yet.

Since the 1930's, increasing use has been made of methods and instruments for measuring social growth and social adjustment. Prominent among these have been the sociograms, sociographs, and related types of procedures and instruments which reveal the nature and degree of the social preferences and attachments of students to their school mates. More effort has been made during this time to discover the personality characteristics of young people—particularly those characteristics of an emotional nature which would throw light upon their behavior in their classroom and in relations with other people in general.

More emphasis is now being placed upon evaluating the product of both tangible and intangible learning activities, such as participation in plays, written compositions, products of the shop and home economics laboratories, and various types of concrete objects.

Also being emphasized more are daily observations of young people in connection with their class work and in their relationships to their fellow students and to adults. It has been pointed out that where team teaching, teaching machines, or programméd learning is employed, the opportunities for such observations and the emphasis upon data obtained from them will be decreased.

There is also a continuing trend to take into consideration the relationship of the student's achievement to his estimated potentiality and to give approval and acknowledgment in terms of the goals set up for the individual.

Plans and Scope of Marking and Reporting

In the early quarter of this century, marking systems were based, at least in theory, upon the apparent fact that in the typical class in which the required learning activities were appropriate for the ability and the status of the class, the measure of achievement of the learners would result in scores distributed in a fashion similar to the normal probability curve.

A negative reaction to this practice set in in the 1920's and continued into the 1930's and well into the 1940's. The use of the normal probability curve came to be regarded as undemocratic and overscientific. This reaction was a part of a general movement against the use of objective tests of achievement, intelligence tests, and statistical methods in general. In some schools the use of conventional marks were abandoned entirely and only "satisfactory" and "unsatisfactory" grades were employed, although sometimes there was the grade of H for outstanding excellence. In some schools the custom of submitting written reports to parents at intervals was abandoned.

But since the early 1950's, this trend has been reversed. The written report card with letter marks of A, B, C, D, E and F is sent home to parents periodically in practically all school systems. In a considerable number of schools, report cards are being sent out less frequently, e.g., every nine weeks. For some time, reports have been submitted to parents on types of growth other than that related closely to high school subjects and on certain qualities of character which the school, along with the home, attempts to develop, such as social growth and personality characteristics.

Because of the rather strong feeling that disapproval should not be given to youngsters who are doing as well as might be expected from indications of their capacity to achieve marks, there was in the 1930's and 1940's a trend toward employing only those marks which were measures of achievement in proportion to the potentiality for achievement. But, this trend was reversed in the 1950's. It has been replaced by a trend toward a dual marking system (recommended by Dr. J. B. Conant in his *American High School Today*) in which one set of marks measures as accurately as possible the absolute achievement of the youngsters and the other set reflects the teacher's best estimates of student's achievement in relation to his capabilities.

Person to Person Avenues of Reporting

In the early 1940's there arose a trend toward reporting to parents in person, either by telephone or in interviews in the school or in the home. In a considerable and an increasing number of schools (principally elementary schools), teachers keep office hours during which parents may confer with them. Furthermore, there has arisen the practice of sending home to parents, not necessarily at any given intervals, some sort of written statement about the student—his progress or lack of progress, his cooperation or lack of cooperation in his work. Teachers tend to emphasize the favorable, particularly in the first few communications.

Testing Programs

Because of the increase in the number of individuals who wish to go to college, the national merit scholarship programs, and the demand for "quality" and "excellence" in learning and teaching, there have developed in the United States—in addition to the college entrance examination board testing programs—some twenty or more national or regional programs.[1] In the past few years,

---

[1] In February, 1962, the American Association of School Administrators, the National Association of Secondary School Principals, and the National Council of Chief State School Officers protested against the multiplicity of testing pro-

school administrators, teachers, students, and parents have protested vigorously against the emphasis upon and the time required for these testing programs. It is argued that more and more teachers are directing their efforts toward good scores on the testing programs rather than toward the achievement of the genuine aims of education. It is also pointed out the scores made on the tests have so little bearing on success in college that they are of little value in predicting college performance and hence in discriminating between good and poor college risks in the borderline areas.[2] The increasing reluctance of administrators to cooperate in more than two of these programs indicates that some plan will soon be worked out for merging the different programs and reducing the time given to them.

BIBLIOGRAPHY

Bates, G. S., "A Two-Way Reporting System," *The Bulletin of the N.A.S.S.P.*, No. 221 (September, 1956), p. 68. School-to-home-to-school reporting.

Brim, R. P., Albert F. Mertz, Jr., and James M. Peebles, "Thorny Problems —How to Weigh Student Marks in Honors Courses," *The Bulletin of the N.A.S.S.P.*, No. 264 (April, 1961), pp. 43–8.

"Call for Halt on Misuse and Overuse of Tests," *The Nation's Schools,* Vol. 67, No. 5 (May, 1961), p. 136.

"Has Testing Gone Too Far?" *National Education Association Journal,* Vol. 62, No. 5 (November, 1959), pp. 15–31.

"High School Record Forms," *The Bulletin of the N.A.S.S.P.*, No. 242 (December, 1958), pp. 236–50.

Morrell, Radcliffe, "Are Your Parent-Teacher Conferences Worthwhile?" *School Management,* Vol. 3, No. 11 (November, 1959), pp. 52–62.

Womer, Frank B., "Pros and Cons of External Testing Programs," *The North Central Association Quarterly,* Vol. 36, No. 2 (Fall, 1961), pp. 201–10. Suggestions for improvement of situation.

---

grams. In a report "Testing, Testing, Testing," submitted by a joint committee, the following recommendations were made: "(1) Develop an overall policy and periodically evaluate the testing program; (2) Evaluate it before you adopt it; (3) Establish equivalency tables, so that a score on one test can be used in lieu of conducting another; (4) Give the tests outside regular class time and without cost to the student; (5) Don't use the scores to compare students, schools, states. The report suggests that use of test scores for publicity purposes by test-makers, test publishers, school administrators, or others should be regarded as an unprofessional practice." *Education U.S.A.,* February 22, 1962, Washington, D.C.: National Education Association.

[2] See "Are Americans Over-Testing?" in *Overview* 2 (August, 1961), 31–33.

CHAPTER IX

Guidance and
Extracurricular Organizations

Guidance

Because of the increased concern about juvenile delinquency, the problems of children from slum areas, and the number of students planning to go to college, there has been a substantial increase in the number of counselors employed in secondary schools. Although most small schools have very limited programs and provide inadequate counseling, more than 16,000 fulltime counselors were engaged in counseling in public secondary schools in 1960–1961.

Staff. In most secondary schools, only those individuals who have had a considerable amount of training are employed as counselors. In general, school administrators insist upon at least one year of graduate work which includes a number of courses in guidance and in fields closely related to guidance. Special certificates for counselors are offered by almost all the states.

Objectives and areas. The fields in which guidance service is offered in secondary schools has been increasing. Guidance is now available for problems of military service, selection of and preparation for college, and various types of personality problems and social adjustment. Counseling is now available for such formerly neglected areas as boy-girl relations, family problems, problems growing out of inability to dress well and lack of at least average physical attractiveness, and social awkwardness and isolation.

It is also being recognized that counseling is appreciated even by those students for whom nothing definite can be done other than to make available a sympathetic listener.

In a small but increasing number of schools, counseling and placement services are also being made available to former students, drop-outs as well as graduates.

Clubs and Other Non-Class Activities

Organization. For several decades there has been much discussion of the advisability of combining the student clubs with the conventional curriculum. Some activities such as band, orchestra, choral singing, glee clubs, debate, dramatics, and publications (to a lesser extent) have become regularly scheduled subjects with credits and marks. But the trend has not been significant in other fields. Nevertheless most extracurricular clubs (except athletic groups) meet during the school day, usually twice a week. On other days, this "activity period" is devoted to scheduled homeroom meetings and assemblies.

Athletics. The unfortunate aspects of overemphasis upon interscholastic athletic competition have been becoming more evident in recent years. The long trips required by such competition, the large number of students going with the teams in automobiles, the undesirable pressures upon the athletic fans, the excessive and distractive excitement of students immediately preceding or immediately following an important game, and the activities involved in recruiting outstanding athletes, have all given rise to increasing concern.

These evils have been spreading at the junior high school level as well, and there is a growing feeling that efforts should be made to reduce these unfortunate effects. More responsibility for formulating and enforcing rules relative to eligibility for athletics and the use of funds received from athletic meets has been delegated to state associations of secondary schools.

Spreading among the schools has been a tendency to insist upon better stewardship and accounting of various kinds of student funds received from exhibition contests as well as from dues. In a large and increasing number of schools an appointed member of the faculty acts as a central bonded treasurer for all such funds and all accounts of students' funds are given an auditing at least once a year and preferably twice a year.

Social life activities. To restrict the growth of undemocratic student social organizations and activities, and to train young people—particularly those coming from the lower economic and cultural levels—in social life activities, increasing attention has been given to providing social events by the schools and providing sponsors for them. There has been a trend toward enlisting the cooperation of parents to act as sponsors and to assist in drawing up, together with the representative of the students and the faculty, principles and rules for governing them.

Essay contests. An increasing number of organizations and firms have been recruiting students to cooperate in a competitive program of writing essays on assigned subjects. These contests have come to be considered undesirable, since they are frequently a device for unwise indoctrination and serve to distract students from their studies. For a period of years the National Association of Secondary School Principals has provided member schools with a body of rules and regulations for participating in essay contests and a list of essay contest projects which have been investigated and approved.

BIBLIOGRAPHY

Brewster, Royce, "Guidance Workers Certification Requirements," U.S. Department of Health, Education and Welfare *Bulletin* No. 14, Washington, D.C.: Office of Education, 1960, 96 pp.

Brown, J. E., and R. A. Dolen, "What Constitutes an Adequate Guidance and Counseling Program for the Junior High School?" *The Bulletin of the N.A.S.S.P.,* No. 255 (April, 1960), pp. 40–4.

Havighurst, Robert J., "Dealing with Problem Youth," *The Nation's Schools,* Vol. 61 (May, 1958), pp. 43–5.

Holt, Charles C., "External Testing Programs," *The Bulletin of the N.A.S.S.P.,* No. 264 (April, 1961), pp. 402–7.

Johnston, Edgar J., Mildred Peters, and Wm. Evraiff, *The Role of the Teacher in Guidance.* Englewood Cliffs, N.J.: Prentice-Hall, Inc., 1959, 275 pp.

Nancarrow, J. E., *et al.,* "Guidance Procedures in the Secondary School," *The Bulletin of the N.A.S.S.P.,* No. 265 (May, 1961), pp. 1–186.

Phillips, Waldo B., "Counselling Negro Pupils—An Educational Dilemma," *Journal of Negro Education,* Vol. 39 (Fall, 1960), pp. 504–7.

Wright, E. W., "Multiple Counselling: Why? When? How?" *Personnel and Guidance Journal,* Vol. 31 (April, 1959), pp. 551–57.

CHAPTER X

Secondary School Organization

Grade-Level Organization

Increased numbers of "reorganized schools." For several decades it has been obvious that the preferred type of grade-level organization of public schools has been the 6-3-3 plan or, in smaller school districts, the 6-6 plan. The necessity for constructing more new school buildings to accommodate the increased enrollments has given opportunity for many districts to change their plan of organization. As a consequence, many schools on the 8-4 plan have shifted to the 6-3-3 or to the 6-6 plan. In many other schools already on the 6-6 plan, enrollments have become sufficiently great so that it was practical for a shift to be made to the 6-3-3 plan. Between 1952 and 1959, the number of junior high schools in the United States increased by more than fifty per cent. In 1959, nearly two-thirds of the school systems of the United States were organized on 6-3-3, 6-2-4, or 6-6 plans and enrolled more than three-fourths of students in grades 9–12.[1]

In 1960 the number of pupils above the sixth grade enrolled in schools on the 6-3-3 plan was 6,700,000; on the 6-6 plan, 5,100,-000; and on the 8-4 plan, 4,200,000. Between 1948 and 1959, 15 per cent of districts established for the first time six-year secondary schools or junior high schools. Secondary school students in districts having some form of junior high schools constituted 82.4 per cent of all students enrolled in secondary schools in 1960.

There is no doubt but that many secondary school districts would have abandoned the 8-4 plan had it not been for the fact that they were separate districts for 4 years of secondary education, especially in Arizona, Illinois, and California. Although slight at present, there is a trend toward school districts providing education for all K-12 years.

---

[1] Based on data in *Public Secondary Schools in the United States,* by Edmond A. Ford and Virgil R. Walker (Washington, D.C.: U.S. Office of Education, 1961).

TABLE 1

NUMBER OF PUBLIC SECONDARY SCHOOLS BY TYPE
OF ORGANIZATION, 1920–1959

	1920		1952		1959	
	No.	Per Cent	No.	Per Cent	No.	Per Cent
Combined Junior-Senior High Schools (6-6)	828	5.8	8,591	36.2	10,130	41.9
Separate Junior High Schools	55	.4	3,227	13.6	4,996	20.6
Senior High Schools (6-3-3)	15	.1	1,021	4.3	1,642	6.8
Reorganized 4-year High Schools (6-2-4)	7	.01	739	3.1	1,396	5.8
Unreorganized 4-year (8-4)	13,421	93.7	10,168	42.8	6,023	24.9
Total	14,326	100.0	23,746	100.0	24,187	100.0

U.S. Office of Education News Release, December 2, 1960.

TABLE 2

ENROLLMENT IN PUBLIC SECONDARY SCHOOLS BY
TYPE OF ORGANIZATION, 1920–1959

	1920		1952		1959	
	No.	Per Cent	No.	Per Cent	No.	Per Cent
Combined Junior-Senior High Schools (6-6)	276,504	13.8	2,696,707	35.1	3,536,921	32.0
Separate Junior High Schools	37,331	1.9	1,526,996	19.8	2,749,602	24.9
Senior High Schools (6-3-3)	11,994	.6	868,848	11.3	1,624,713	14.7
Reorganized 4-year High Schools (6-2-4)	5,797	.3	659,158	8.6	1,193,518	10.8
Unreorganized 4-year (8-4)	1,667,480	83.4	1,937,210	25.2	1,939,365	17.6
Total	1,999,106	100.0	7,688,919	100.0	11,044,119	100.0

U.S. Office of Education News Release, December 2, 1960.

Other types of organization. In the last ten or twelve years, summer school offerings have been expanded and enrollments greatly increased. Summer school attendance has been encouraged by the scarcity of summer employment, the desire to reduce the number of subject failures in high school, and the opportunity for brighter students to complete their secondary school education a year earlier. Also, more school districts are providing secondary school courses in the evening.

School Size

Trend toward larger schools. The number of small secondary schools has been very greatly reduced. Whereas in 1930 the median enrollment in four-year high schools in the United States was approximately 125 students, the corresponding figure for 1958–1959 was approximately 250 students and is steadily increasing. According to the U.S. Office of Education, the number of secondary schools enrolling less than 200 students has decreased to approximately 40% by 1961. There has been no increase in the number of schools enrolling more than 2,500 students: the growth is in the number of schools enrolling between 500 and 1,000 students. This increase has resulted partly from an increase in population, partly from the larger proportion of students staying on through grades 10 through 12 and partly from the movement toward consolidation which has been accelerated since 1950, especially in Illinois, Colorado, Wisconsin, and Iowa. Extension of transportation facilities has also contributed to the abandonment of small secondary schools and the establishment of centrally located larger ones.[2] Between 1938 and 1958, the number of school districts in the United States decreased from 117,410 to 48,043. In Iowa, for example, there were 4,417 districts and 819 secondary schools in 1954 and 1955, while in 1961–1962 there were only 1,390 districts with 510 high schools.

In a number of states—Arkansas, Kentucky, Kansas, Louisiana, Nebraska, Mississippi, North Carolina, North Dakota, Oklahoma, South Dakota, Vermont, and Wyoming—the consolidation movement has proceeded very slowly and, as a result, many secondary schools in these states, especially segregated secondary schools for Negroes, are too small to provide anything but relatively inferior programs and facilities for secondary education.

Optimum size of high school. Increased attention has been given in recent years to the optimum size of high schools. Dr. J. B. Conant, for example, recommends that wherever possible secondary schools be established with at least 100 students in the twelfth

---

[2] In 1958, 11,343,132 pupils were transported to school at public expense. Nearly five million of these were secondary school students. By 1960–1961, the number of school districts in the United States had decreased from 83,614 in 1950–1951 to 37,115, less than half. *N.E.A. Research Bulletin*, 39 (February, 1961), p. 28.

grade. This recommendation is made not only for the purpose of increasing the offerings of the school and the quality and extent of better housing and equipment, but also to encourage the formation of groups of definitely superior students and groups of definitely less academically able students. The consensus of leaders of secondary education based on data gathered in the doctoral theses of

TABLE 3

PER CENT OF PUBLIC SECONDARY SCHOOLS
BY SIZE OF ENROLLMENT, 1938–1959

Enrollment Interval	1938	1952	1959
Less than 50	17.9	11.5	5.8
50–74	12.2	9.7	6.1
75–99	10.6	8.8	6.2
100–199	25.6	25.4	21.5
200–299	10.2	13.0	14.0
300–499	9.1	13.0	16.5
500–999	7.7	11.6	18.7
1,000–2,499	5.7	6.5	10.9
2,500 or more	1.00	.45	.71
Total number of schools	25,057	23,746	24,187

U.S. Office of Education News Release, December 2, 1960.

Professors Albert I. Oliver, Jr., and W. C. Wood at the University of Colorado, and Dr. L. P. Mennozi, at the University of Denver, seems to indicate a preference for secondary schools of the following sizes: two-year junior high schools, 300 to 500 students; three-year junior high schools, 500 to 800 students; senior high schools, 600 to 1,000 students; and four-year high schools, 800 to 1,200 students.

Schools-within-a-school. Concern about the depersonalization of the relationship among students and between student and teacher in the large secondary schools has given rise to a trend toward "the school-within-a-school." This type of organization, adopted in an increasing number of larger secondary schools, attempts to restore at least to some degree the personal acquaintance and relations common in the smaller schools. It divides the larger school into two, three, or four units with somewhat separate educational faculties, student bodies, and housing facilities. Each smaller unit tends to maintain its own identity to some extent; teachers get better acquainted with the students in the unit and students become better acquainted with each other.

Improving small schools. Increased attention is being given to improving the quality of education in the small school.[3] In many sparsely settled areas—particularly in the Rocky Mountains—transportation to larger schools is impossible for part of the year by reason of snow and road conditions. Some of the devices being employed to solve this problem are correspondence courses, co-operative arrangements whereby the services of teachers, counselors, and health and physical examiners, and others are shared by several schools. In a few states, notably New York, this practice is recognized by law.

Trend Toward Desegregated and Non-Public Schools

Desegregated schools. Following the Supreme Court decision in 1954, the number of schools segregated on the basis of race or color and the percentage of boys and girls attending such schools has steadily decreased in all states except Mississippi, Virginia, Louisiana, Arkansas, and South Carolina. In Tennessee, North Carolina, Kentucky, and Texas the decrease has been substantial, while in Georgia, Alabama, and Florida a beginning has been made. There is every reason to believe that this trend will continue, and probably at a somewhat accelerated pace.

As of February, 1960, 748 of the 6,973 school districts in seventeen southern states and the District of Columbia had been desegregated. These desegregated schools served 3,044,070 pupils of a total public school population in the districts of 12,940,443.[4]

This trend presents the problem of adapting instruction to the needs and interests of the Negro students who have for the most part attended inferior schools and are therefore behind white children who have attended better schools.

Non-public schools. The number of non-public secondary schools and the number of secondary school students attending them has

---

[3] "Rural Renaissance—Revitalizing Small High Schools," *Bulletin* (Washington, D.C.: U.S. Office of Education, 1961), No. 11, by Edmund R. Ford.

[4] Reported from the *NEA Research Bulletin* 39 (February, 1961), pp. 26–31. As reported in *Education News and World Report,* December 4, 1961, mixed schools often tend to become unmixed again.

risen in recent years. The increased financial prosperity of American families has not only made it possible for them to send their children to schools charging tuition but also has made it possible for them to donate gifts and to make bequests for the establishment and support of denominational secondary schools. Many parents have come to feel that their children—particularly those with superior capacity for learning—were not achieving up to their potentiality and should be sent to schools in which special attention would be given bright students and greater emphasis placed to intellectual objectives.[5]

In view of the increase in juvenile delinquency and the concentration upon sex, violence, and materialism in movies and television, many parents have preferred to send their children to schools stressing religious and spiritual values.

Leaders in the Catholic church have pressed, with increasing vigor, for public funds or services in connection with textbooks and transportation. In a few states concessions of this nature have been legalized and implemented. Many Catholic leaders have taken a positive position that Federal funds, if provided for public schools, should be available to non-public schools. This position has contributed heavily to the failure of Congress to provide general Federal aid to the schools.

Another factor contributing to the increasing enrollments of non-public secondary schools has been the desire on the part of a larger number of parents for their boys and girls to have a college education[6] and a consequence preference for a secondary school which would concentrate heavily upon preparation for college or at least for passing college board examinations and other testing programs having to do with admission to college, scholarships, and

[5] Studies over a period of several decades have shown that, especially at Ivy League colleges, graduates from public high schools do as well or better in scholarship as do graduates from non-public secondary schools. In recent years larger proportions of the students of selective colleges for women come from public high schools—e.g., in 1961, Mt. Holyoke, 72%; Barnard, 69%; Smith, 59%; Wellesley, 58%; Vassar, 55%; and Radcliff, 53%.

[6] In 1960, 30 per cent of all boys and girls in the United States (one half of all graduated) went to college, as compared to 10 per cent in Russia and less than 5 per cent in England. In 1960 the percentage of students in Ivy League colleges and universities who were graduates of public high schools had exceeded 50 per cent.

fellowships. The percentage of secondary school students attending non-public schools has risen from 10 per cent to a little more than 14 per cent.

Some non-public secondary schools are established primarily to carry on experimental programs of secondary education. As indicated in a brochure on non-public schools by David Mallory,[7] the amount of experimentation in non-public schools has increased greatly and has involved a wide variety of problems. A slight trend (one rare instance is at Ottawa, Ohio) is the merging of the local public and parochial high schools.

In the past few years, a few districts have arranged for some parochial school students to take courses in science, mathematics and foreign languages in the public secondary schools.

Comprehensive Secondary Schools

With few exceptions, secondary schools in the United States, have been devoted to general education rather than to specialized areas. There has recently developed a demand for establishment of specialized high schools, especially schools for the very bright students. Nevertheless, all but a few American educators have vigorously defended the comprehensive high schools and apparently the great majority of the American public will continue to go along with them.

Support and Control of Public Education

Financial support.[8] Since 1930 there has been a shift in the support of public elementary and secondary schools from local to state and Federal funds. In 1930, one per cent of all funds for elementary and secondary schools came from Federal sources, 20 per cent from state sources, and 80 per cent from local taxes. In 1960 four times as much support came from Federal funds, twice as much from state funds, and only a little more than half from local taxes. A greater increase in the proportion of local funds is taking place in states in which the percentage of funds from local

---

[7] *New Approaches in Education* (Boston, Mass.: National Council of Independent Schools, 1961), 192 pp.

[8] Data presented here are from *N.E.A. Research Bulletin*, Vol. 39, No. 1 (February, 1961).

sources had previously been much smaller than the average for the nation. (In 1960, slightly less than four per cent of personal income was spent for public elementary and secondary education as compared to approximately three per cent in 1940.)

Control. Control of public secondary schools continues to be exercised chiefly by the authorities in the communities in which the schools are located rather than by the state or Federal government. Nevertheless, the National Defense Education Act (passed in 1958), with subsidies for instruction in science, foreign language, mathematics and guidance, provides a new type of Federal influence on the curriculum of secondary schools. It is comparable to that exercised for a half century through Federal subsidies to vocational schools whose programs met the standards set up by the United States Office of Education.[9]

The increased amount of state support for education has resulted only in a very slight increase of state influence over secondary schools. Each state accredits schools in its domain but exercises very little control over the funds.

The regional accrediting associations continue to exercise little actual control even over accredited schools although it has considerable influence over the curriculum, training of staff, equipment, and administrative relationships in borderline schools. One notable development has been the raising of subject matter requirements for teachers in schools accredited by the North Central Association of Colleges and Secondary Schools.

Cooperative planning. There has continued the trend toward cooperative procedure in decision-making relative to courses of study and other aspects of secondary school programs. Not only teachers, but students and the public as well, are participating in such decisions. The role of lay people in this connection is invariably advisory.

Length of School Year, Day, and Week

Longer school year. There has been much discussion in recent years of the practicability of having students attend school through-

---

[9] In 1960–1961, more than 21 million dollars was distributed for instructional equipment and materials.

out the year, thereby making use of school buildings which for the
most part lie idle for three months of the year. Although a few
schools, notably Aliquipa, Pennsylvania, in the 1920's, have ex-
perimented with such programs in which students are required to
attend three of four quarters, the trend has been relatively insignifi-
cant. The trend is likely to continue as a large number of parents
wish to take their children with them on vacations and the climate
in summer in many regions in the United States is not favorable for
attendance at school. Much more common is the provision for
various types of recreational and supplementary educational opportunities in the summer for students of secondary school age. By
1960 the proportion of urban school districts operating summer
schools had increased by approximately one-half. The median length
of the summer term had increased to 7.3 weeks.[10]

There has been a slow but steady trend toward lengthening the
school year. The median length of the school year has increased
from approximately 165 days in 1930 to 178 days in 1960 with
more and more schools remaining open for 180 days a year, as
compared to 185 to 200 days in major countries in Europe. Twelve-
month employment for teachers was reported by 5.2 per cent of
the urban school districts in 1958–1959. A growing number of
schools employ teachers on a ten-month basis.

Longer school days. There is also a trend to lengthen the school
day. The distractions of television and a highly developed social
life, and the lack of suitable study facilities at home, have led a
growing number of schools to add from 20 to 45 minutes to the
school day.[11]

Some secondary schools have added a "zero" or "early-bird"
period before the conventional opening time in the morning. In
regions where daylight comes a little later in the morning and stays
a little later in the afternoon, an extra period of 40 or 45 minutes
has been added in the afternoon.

In 1958–1959 only 1.4 per cent of secondary school pupils were
on half day sessions, the situation being worst in Connecticut (8.9
per cent) and New York (6.1 per cent).

---

[10] *N.E.A. Research Bulletin,* Vol. 39, No. 1 (February, 1961).

[11] In a few schools, the library is now kept open for study in the afternoons,
evenings, or Saturday mornings.

Longer school week. In practically all schools where an extra period has been added, and the school day lengthened by that much, only elective subjects or duplicate sections of subjects are offered. Although secondary schools in most other countries operate at least five and one-half days per week, the practice in this country has been confined to discussion and to a very small number of schools on an experimental basis. In a few districts, action has been taken toward lengthening the school week; some classes at least being held on Saturday, usually in the morning.

A very small number of schools are trying a four-day school week but only on an experimental basis.

Class Period, Class Size, and Daily Schedule

Length of class period. For almost a half century there has been a steady increase in the length of class periods—from approximately 40 minutes net to 55 minutes and in a few schools to 90 minutes. This shift has resulted largely from the desire to concentrate learning activities in the classroom rather than in the study halls. In an increasing number of secondary schools, particularly junior high schools, there has been a trend toward the "double-period block of time" to provide flexibility and to make it easier to make excursions outside the school.

Number of periods. For several decades junior high schools have been shifting from an eight- or nine-period day to a six- or a seven-period day. In the past few years the trend has been definitely toward the seven-period day, thus enabling the school to carry on a somewhat richer program of electives and to provide two periods in the week for club activities and for study in the library.

Class size. Because of the shortage of teachers and the shortage of funds to increase teachers' salaries, there was in the 1940's a very small increase in the average size of class sections. In many secondary schools today, particularly junior high schools, approximately half of the class sections are composed of more than thirty students. This trend has probably spent itself as it has encountered increasing opposition from teachers and administrators; nevertheless, the publicity given the team teaching plan with classes of 100 to 150 students and the continued shortage of teachers and school funds, indicates further experimentation with some sort of large class teaching may well be expected.

As a result of the emphasis on the ability to write English correctly and effectively, there has been a trend in the direction of reducing the number of students in classes in English.

The lunch period. Over the years the number of schools providing cafeteria service and the percentage of students eating at school has increased so that almost all secondary schools provide a short lunch period. Increased enrollment has made it necessary for most schools to provide two and sometimes three staggered lunch periods. In 1959–1960, more than 13.5 million children in public and non-profit schools were participating in the national school lunch program.[12]

Fewer class meetings. For the past few years a small number of secondary schools—particularly three- and four-year and senior high schools—have operated on a schedule in which the classes in the so-called "solid subjects" have met four times a week instead of five times. This shift has been confined almost entirely to schools with a long class period; it has been most prominent in Connecticut and California, though it is slowly spreading throughout the country. The general report is that the students do as well or almost as well in classes meeting four times a week as they did previously in classes meeting five times a week.

BIBLIOGRAPHY

Campbell, W. H., "Summer High School Survey," *The Bulletin of the N.A.S.S.P.,* No. 254 (March, 1960), pp. 44–9.

"Desegregation Report," *Education Digest,* 27–3 (November, 1961), pp. 55–7. From Civil Rights Report No. 2, Washington, D.C.: U.S. Government Printing Office, 1961.

Diamond, Hugh J., "In Naskayuna a 'House' Fits Into an Existing School," *The Nation's Schools,* Vol. 67, No. 12 (June, 1961), pp. 68–9, 94.

Dulstead, William M., "How Can Summer School Improve the Total School Program?" *The Bulletin of the N.A.S.S.P.,* No. 237 (April, 1958), pp. 31–6.

Fogg, Walter F., "The Scarsdale Plan is Flexible and Relaxed," *The Nation's Schools,* No. 12 (June, 1961), pp. 66–8.

---

[12] *N.E.A. Research Bulletin,* Vol. 39, No. 1 (February, 1961).

Martin, Clyde V., Wm. E. Fogg, and George D. Stephen, "Segregation vs. Desegregation," *Phi Delta Kappan*, Vol. XLI, No. 7 (April, 1960), pp. 319–23.

Robinson, W. A., "The Problem of Integration in the Phoenix Schools," *The Journal of Negro Education*, XXV (Fall, 1959), pp. 371–79.

CHAPTER XI

Secondary School Housing
and Instructional Equipment

The increase in secondary school enrollment and population mobility since 1950 has resulted in a substantial increase in the number of new secondary school buildings. The construction of new secondary school buildings accelerated in the late 1950's and early 1960's and will probably continue throughout the 1960's and the 1970's. The building of these new schools has given many opportunities for experimentation.

New Types of Buildings

In the 1930's there originated a trend toward construction of one-story buildings without stairways. Closely related to this has been the trend toward "campus housing"—the development of several units of housing on a large site.

New shapes of buildings. School buildings and classrooms have traditionally been rectangular. In recent years, however, there have appeared a number of different shapes and sizes: round buildings, semicircular buildings, oval buildings, triangular, quadrangular, pentangular, and hexangular, and indeed a few octangular buildings. A number of new buildings contain six to eight trapezoidal classrooms arranged in a hexagon or octagon with a central enclosed room for audio-visual materials and equipment.

Many educators believe that these types of buildings fit educational programs better. The cost is less rather than more than that of the more traditional building.

Building units. In recent years a number of large secondary schools has been constructed in the form of several units—for example, a unit for science, a unit for humanities, a unit for shops, and a unit for administrative offices.

Installment building. Some secondary school buildings are be-

79

ing constructed in installments, the idea being to provide for the number of students likely to be enrolled in the next few years and to put off the completion of the building until more students enroll. Thus the tax load and interest are postponed for at least a few years. Even in such buildings, however, the auditorium, cafeteria, library, gymnasium, and other central units are planned to accommodate as many students as will eventually be enrolled in the completed building.

Some prefabricated school buildings are also being constructed. This type of building is not only usually more flexible with respect to size of classrooms but it is the type to which additions may be built more easily. In most instances, the total cost is usually less.

New Types of Rooms and Equipment

Classroom size. More large rooms are being included, particularly in those schools which plan to have team teaching and large lecture groups. More small rooms are also being provided for small discussion groups. Furthermore, in many new schools provision has been for the easy conversion of conventional classrooms into those of larger or smaller size.

Shapes of classrooms. The shape of the new classroom, traditionally rectangular, may now be triangular, semicircular, pentangular, trapezoidal or oval.

New types of instructional rooms. In recent years secondary school buildings have been constructed or modified to include language laboratories,[1] special science rooms, and special rooms for dramatics, band, and choral groups and business machines. Facilities for both radio and television broadcasting (including production studios) have also been included in many new buildings or set up in old buildings.

New types of non-instructional rooms. Many new buildings include units which have multiple use, such as "cafetorium" and in a few "cafeteria-library." Many of the new schools provided special

---

[1] The U.S. Office of Education recently stated that whereas there were only about 60 language laboratories in secondary schools in the United States in 1958, there were approximately 3,000 in 1961. In some schools these laboratories are used for music and speech, as well as for foreign languages.

rooms for housing audio-visual materials and machines as well as printed materials. In many of the new buildings, too, there are more office and conference rooms for counselors, health programs and administrative assistants.

Other trends. With the greater use of overhead lighting, increased attention has been given to the construction of buildings with at least some interior, windowless rooms.[2] Some administrators have been courageous enough to plan buildings with no windows at all.

It might be noted in passing that there is a trend toward using school buildings for educational, recreational, and social purposes by adults and former students.

School Sites

Larger sites. In the 1940's there arose a trend toward the construction of secondary school buildings on large sites—for example, junior high schools on sites from 15 to 30 acres, and the senior high school on a site of 20 to 40 acres. This trend has been somewhat accelerated in recent years.

Non-central location. Unless great expense is involved, the larger sites must be in undeveloped parts of the city and this has resulted in the construction of more and more school buildings on locations that are not central. With the development of public school transportation, the increase in the number of young people driving cars, and the trend toward eating lunch at school, the objections to such sites has diminished.

Space for parking. Many new schools are providing parking space, limited to use by teachers and by those students who are physically handicapped or who live far from the school. Although some schools provide ample parking space for all students who wish to drive, a considerable number of schools maintain that students who are well able to walk and who live at short distances from school should not be given permission permits to drive on the school grounds and should be discouraged from driving to and from school. This reduces the danger of automobile accidents by

---

[2] At least one high school, at Hobbs, New Mexico, is being built underground with no natural light or ventilation.

student drivers, and the temptation to students to cut classes or study halls and to lounge or drive about in their cars.

Major Equipment

Audio-visual education equipment. Major equipment being installed more commonly in recent years includes audio-visual equipment—particularly overhead projector, television reception sets and television broadcasting equipment, tape recorders, and film collections. A few school systems have video-tape machines which record television programs for later use. The present expense of the video-tape machine prohibits its use in smaller or less well-financed schools.[3]

Teaching machines. Expenditures for teaching machines have also risen in recent years. In many schools teaching machines have been purchased to be used principally in the central offices or teachers' rooms for the purpose of scoring tests and only in limited fashion in instruction.

Sorting machines and computers. In a number of schools, especially larger ones in well-to-do districts, sorting machines and computers have been purchased and made available to the staff. These machines are used for a wide variety of bookkeeping and educational accounting purposes, in schedule construction and student programming to carry on research and investigations, and to prepare reports to the board of education and the public.

BIBLIOGRAPHY

"An Architectural Solution to the Junior High School Buildings," *School Management*, Vol. 4, No. 11 (November, 1960), pp. 101–8. Diagrams and discussion of new ideas.

Clinchy, Evans, *Profiles of Significant Schools: Wayland Senior High School, Wayland, Massachusetts.* New York: Educational Facilities Laboratories, 1960, 28 pp.

Colbert, Charles R., "Perception Core School," *The Nation's Schools*, Vol. 65, No. 9 (March, 1960), pp. 79–87.

Design for ETV—Planning for Schools with Television. New York: Educational Facilities Laboratories, 1960, 96 pp.

---

[3] Dr. Robert E. deKieffer, Director of the Bureau of Audio-Visual Instruction of the University of Colorado (in a letter under date of November 17, 1961), points out that the ampex video tape machine costs approximately $45,000.

"Getting Away from the Rectangular Classroom," *School Management,* Vol. 8 (July, 1960), pp. 60–6.

Hardman, B. Reede, and Philip Lones, "Two-story Circular Buildings and Trapezoidal Classrooms Offer Unique Advantages," *The Nation's Schools,* Vol. 68, No. 1 (July, 1960), pp. 50–6.

Jones, J. Wilbert, "How to Plan Lighting for a New School," *School Management,* Vol. 4, No. 11 (November, 1960), pp. 64–6.

Price, J. W., "More Experience with Utilizing a New School Plant at Syosset, New York, in Contributing to Staff Use and Curriculum Development," *The Bulletin of the N.A.S.S.P.,* No. 243 (January, 1959), pp. 167–80.

Twiford, Don D., "Physical Facilities for School Guidance Services," U.S. Department of Health, Education and Welfare (Washington, D.C.: Office of Education, 1959). Suggestions for offices, equipment.

CHAPTER XII

School-Community Relationships

Increased Need for Better Relationships

Increased costs. One of the most pronounced trends in American education in the past two decades has been toward the expansion and improvement of relationships between the school and its personnel, and between the school and the community. This development has been greatly stimulated by the need for a large amount of additional housing and for nearly twice as many teachers as before the close of World War II. School authorities have been compelled to ask the public for greatly increased financial support. Expenditures on the public elementary and secondary schools in the United States was only about 3.5 billion dollars in the early 1940's, but the budget for 1961–1962 was 14.3 billion dollars (not including 3.5 billion dollars for capital outlay and interest).

The drive for more funds also stimulated the necessity to pay teachers much larger salaries to offset the increased cost of living and the competition of government and industry for college graduates, and the increased desire of the public in general for improvement in the quality of education.

Changes in secondary education. There is also a very great need for better public relations in order that the public may understand the changing program of the schools. The public has been confused by these changes, and administrators and educators have recognized the necessity for encouraging closer contact and supplying better information.

Criticisms of the schools. The need for better public relations has been increased by the vigor and variety of the criticisms of American public education. These criticisms, although they have unfortunately given rise to much confusion, have also stimulated the public's desire to know more about the schools.

Avenues and Means of Better Public Relations

The student. Much attention has been given to improving public relations through the students themselves. Educators have long realized that parents are more influenced by their own children than by any other source of information about the schools. Consequently, in recent years attempts have been made to acquaint the students themselves with what is going on in the schools, to allow them to participate more in making decisions about school activities, and efforts to improve the amount and quality of health, guidance, and other services available to them.

Publications. There has been a very definite improvement in the amount and the quality of press releases. In most school districts, administrators have developed very definite systems for feeding news releases to the press. Indeed, in some school districts an assistant to the superintendent is responsible for publicity through the local papers and in many he has lieutenants in each of the schools who not only assist in preparing the releases but also make sure that the flow of fresh news tips continues.

Many schools now send parents an occasional mimeographed or printed bulletin about the work of the school. The accounts are written simply and with brevity and deal primarily with the things in which parents are interested or in which the educators believe they can become interested. New developments and the progress of new developments, as well as progress and achievements of the schools, are included in the program of contents for such publication together with occasional statements of needs of the schools.

Face-to-face conferences. Educators have been coming to realize that face-to-face conferences are much more effective than other types of communication and that they have peculiar values particularly in the matter of developing good personal relationships and good will which can be capitalized on for the benefits of the school and its program.

In an increasing number of schools, teachers designate office hours and parents are encouraged to come in and to talk over the problems of the student and the program of the school.

Many of the schools continue to have "School Visitation Day" or "School Visitation Night." Perhaps the most rapidly increasing type and probably the most effective is the "Go to School Night," when the parents visit the various teachers and classrooms on the schedule followed by their children with periods only a fraction of the length of the regular class period. The counselors, administrators, supervisors, and other officials are available for conference and parents are encouraged, indeed urged, to see them. Refreshments are usually served.

Also increasing in recent years, although more commonly in the elementary school than in the secondary school, is the use of home visits. Many parents will not or cannot visit the school. Where there are core programs or homeroom programs, teachers are usually expected to visit the homes of most if not all their students fairly early in the school year. The use of visiting teachers began some twenty or thirty years ago and has spread in recent years. In view of the results obtained in many cities, notably Detroit, in the form of better understanding of and more favorable attitudes toward schools and their personnel, this type of service to the community will most likely be employed by more and more schools.

Community life of educators. It has become increasingly recognized that social, business and other contacts of all members of the staff—administrators, supervisors, counselors, teachers, secretaries, and custodians—in the community have potential value for developing and improving public relations. Because this is true, there has been an increased amount of attention given to keeping all members of the staff, including secretarial and custodial staff, informed about new developments in the programs and the problems of the school.

There has also developed the feeling that educators should avoid participating in community controversies or becoming members of controversial groups except in cases where the controversy involves the welfare of the students and of the school. The number of educators belonging to community service clubs has greatly increased in recent years.

Special contacts with low cultural groups. Havighurst, Stiles, Conant, Brownell, and others have recognized that juvenile crime and education-impeding characteristics thrive in those sections of cities where families of low cultural and economic status or unassimilated ethnic origins tend to congregate. In Detroit and in a small but increasing number of metropolitan districts, for example, programs have developed which link the parents with the school and with the cultural life of the community as a whole.

Home visits have been combined with efforts to bring the parents of such families to the school for recreational and learning programs of adult education. As a result, the children seem to be less susceptible to juvenile delinquency and more interested in their school work. They are making better grades in their classes and creating fewer problems such as absenteeism, group and individual quarrels, insubordination, and discourteous treatment to teachers.

Adult education and the use of buildings. Secondary buildings and members of secondary school faculties are being used to provide more educational and recreational programs not only for older people, but also for recent graduates and drop-outs. As interest in the programs grows and their scope and utility widens, buildings and members of the secondary school staff are being employed more fully in evenings, on Saturdays, and summer vacations. The contacts thus made are useful in developing better attitudes in the community and conveying more accurate information about the schools.

Cooperation with parents in the matter of students' school records. There is also a trend to permit parents under certain conditions to see the school records of their children. This trend has been accelerated by the recommendation of a special committee headed by Dean John H. Fischer of Teachers College at Columbia University, appointed by James E. Allen, Jr., Commissioner of Education, New York State.

To avoid misuse of this information, the committee recommends that schools be instructed to distinguish more clearly between school records, background data which teachers use to prepare records, and communications which cooperating agencies furnish to inform and advise the school staff. It adds that

> Such distinctions appear to be possible within present statutory limitations, but if they are not, we recommend that appropriate corrective steps be taken to legalize these distinctions for they seem to be urgently required in order to protect the welfare of the children of the state.[1]

---

[1] *Saturday Review,* November 18, 1961, pp. 45–46.

BIBLIOGRAPHY

Airnick, Sylvia, *et al.,* "Public Relations for the American High School," *The Bulletin of the N.A.S.S.P.,* No. 257 (September, 1960), 137 pp.

Beck, Robert H., Mrs. Dollin Brown, Harold L. Clapp, and Benjamin C. Walter, "The Meaning of Quality in Education—A Symposium," North Central Association Quarterly (Summer, 1961).

Bullock, Robert P., "Power Elite in the Community," *The School Executive* (March, 1959), pp. 59–61. Discusses the use of influential people in good public relations.

Conant, James B., *Slums and Suburbs.* New York: McGraw-Hill Book Co., 1961.

Cuony, Edward R., "Student-Parent-Teacher Conferences," *The Bulletin of the N.A.S.S.P.,* No. 226 (February, 1958), pp. 180–87. Discusses techniques and results.

Rice, Arthur H., "Planned Propaganda," *The Nation's Schools,* Vol. 60, No. 4 (October, 1957), pp. 98–102, 150–52.

Silberman, Charles E., "The Public Business: The Remaking of American Education," *Fortune* (April, 1961), pp. 3–11.

"Ten Criticisms of Public Education," *National Education Association Research Bulletin,* Vol. 35, No. 4 (December, 1957).

The Classroom Teacher and Public Relations, Washington, D.C.: National Education Association, 1959, 49 pp.

CHAPTER XIII

The Education and
Growth of Teachers

In spite of the shortage of qualified secondary school teachers, progress is being made in improving standards for certification and raising the standards for employment. Nevertheless, it has become necessary for urban districts to employ more and more teachers with little or no experience. Even the wealthiest urban districts are forced to employ teachers with less experience than previously.

In all secondary schools, the increased number of unqualified teachers and teachers of little experience, the changes called for in the curriculum and in methods of instruction as well as in measurement, counselling, and supervision of extra-curricular activities, have given rise to a need for staff supervision and assistance.

Standards of Preparation and Certification

The classroom teacher. There has been a growing demand for the general cultural education of elementary and secondary school teachers. This general education must be in addition to adequate subject matter background in the subjects taught and adequate professional preparation for the types of responsibilities which teachers are asked to assume.

Slowly, but observedly, teachers' colleges and departments of education in universities have incorporated in their curricula for prospective teachers appropriate general education courses—especially in basic physical and biological science, including geology, history, English, and in economics, political science, sociology, and anthropology. Especially valuable and increasingly prescribed as preferred are comprehensive general education courses, e.g., in social sciences.

There has also been a shift in the direction of encouraging, if not requiring, the prospective teacher to take courses which are related to the present day culture and problems as opposed to concentration upon conventional academic or cultural courses.

In an increasing number of colleges and universities, basic comprehensive courses in physical science, biological science, social studies, history, literature, and English language are being offered, if not required, for the general education of all college and university students.

Some critics of the professional education of teachers and administrators have focused upon and grossly exaggerated the lack of general education. These critics have sometimes made exaggerated statements and unwarranted generalizations. They usually complain about what is called an excess amount of course work in "methods." Many of the most vocal critics inaccurately, and probably ignorantly, classify as methods all courses in education, including those in the history of education, introduction to education in the United States, educational psychology, measurement and research, guidance and counselling, secondary education, the curriculum and educational sociology.

But the criticism has stimulated and accelerated the trend toward improving the appropriate general education of teachers and administrators. Attention has been profitably directed toward the desirability of the general education of teachers in areas which serve as background to teaching and education in general and to certain intellectual disciplines. According to a recently released statement by Professor Earl J. McGrath, Institute of Higher Education, Teachers College, Columbia University, 36 per cent of the studies of prospective secondary school teachers are general or liberal studies. Professor McGrath has observed that on the average only one-sixth of the courses taken by prospective secondary school teachers are professional courses. Several times that proportion is devoted to professional courses by prospective doctors, attorneys, engineers, pharmacists, music, and business specialists.

Except in a few institutions, the amount of work required in education has not decreased. In a great majority of teachers' colleges and liberal arts colleges, careful investigation has been under way to reduce the amount of undesirable duplication and to strengthen the professional courses offered. Since secondary school teachers participate in the supervision of clubs and extracurricular activities, in counseling and guidance, in textbook selection and course-of-study construction, in public relations, and in a number of other fields, there has been a slow trend to incorporate more training in these areas.

In a large and increasing number of urban districts, a year's preparation for teaching—beyond the bachelor's degree—is required for appointment as a standard teacher.

An observable trend toward more effective subject matter specialization of secondary school teachers may be seen by the fact that many teachers' colleges, liberal arts colleges, and universities are providing for a broader rather than an intensive major. For example, in an increasing number of schools it is possible to major in a combination of history and social sciences with courses in various fields of history, sociology, economics, political science, and geography; and to major in science, with courses in physics, chemistry, biology, and mathematics, rather than an intense major in one of these fields and an inadequate minor in one or more others. The trend has not been so great in the fields of foreign languages and English.

In practically all urban districts, additional salary is given teachers possessing a master's degree,[1] and in many for a year of graduate work even without a master's degree. In districts of more than 5,000 population throughout the United States the great majority of secondary school teachers have had five years of preparation; in many districts all of them.

In the past few years a number of states have revised the legislation, procedures, and standards of certification for teaching in the secondary schools so as to require five years of college work with specified preparation in certain professional responsibilities such as practice teaching, methods of teaching, growth and development or psychology of adolescents, and introduction to secondary education. In most of the states which require five years of preparation it is still possible for college graduates to obtain a certificate which ordinarily is good for three years during which time the holder is expected to complete the requirements for the professional certifi-

---

[1] *Education U.S.A.*, National Public Schools Relation Association, N.E.A. (November 16, 1961), p. 4.

cate. In a majority of the states the temporary certificate may not be renewed.

In the fall of 1961, the Council of Chief State School Officers in Baltimore recommended that the standard of five years of preparation be adopted for secondary school teachers immediately and for elementary school teachers in the near future.

Counselors. The number of states providing special certification for counselors has been gradually increasing for the past two or three decades. In recent years a few of the states have come to require a special certificate for those participating in the program on a part- or full-time basis. For certification as a counselor, at least five years of college and university work is almost always required. This work must include, in addition to several courses in guidance and counseling, courses in mental hygiene, adolescence, psychometry, personality and its measurement, and sociology.

The increase in the number of counselors in secondary schools in the United States has been accelerated by the publicity given Dr. J. B. Conant's recommendation (in *American High School Today*) that one full-time counselor be available for every 250 or 300 students.[2] The increased number of students planning to go to college, the increased number of students of inferior interests and ability in academic subjects going on through senior high school, and the increased number of problems created by compulsory military service, juvenile delinquency, and slum conditions have contributed to the need for more intensive and extensive counseling and guidance.

Administrators and supervisors. In recent years there have been added to the staff of the superintendent of schools one or more assistant superintendents or directors. Most prominent among these has been assistant superintendents in charge of buildings and construction, assistant superintendents in charge of instruction, business managers, directors of secondary education, supervisors, coordinators, or "helping" teachers in various areas such as English, social studies, science, and mathematics.

Vice-principals or other assistant administrators are more fre-

---

[2] Many administrators are now building up their staff counselors to the ratio of one to every 350 students in junior high schools and one to every 250 students in senior high schools.

quently provided in the secondary schools and given responsibility in a particular field, such as student organization, guidance and counseling, curriculum and instruction, or attendance and records.

Principals in all but the very smallest and weakest secondary schools have master's degrees. In 1962, 44 states provided a special certificate for secondary school principals or administrators in general. However, only 9 states in 1962 required the principal to have such a certificate.

The requirements for the principal's certificate vary from state to state and is changing with time. All but a few require a year of graduate work, usually with a major in education for a master's degree. Many specify courses or credit hours in certain fields such as secondary education and school administration and supervision. All require at least two years, usually three, of teaching experience.

In an increasing number of states, a provisional certificate is provided for assistant principals who lack the full requirements. This may be replaced by a professional certificate after the completion of the required professional preparation and experience.

In recent years there has been a trend toward expecting the administrators of large high schools and superintendents of schools to have a sixth year of preparation. After January, 1964, to be accepted, new applicants for membership in the American Association of School Administrators must have two years of preparation beyond a bachelor's degree.[3]

Staff Leadership and In-Service Growth

Cooperative group procedure. There has also been a strong tendency to increase the amount of in-service professional growth activities of the teachers. More schools are conducting institutes or workshops before and/or after the opening of the school term, and more local boards of education are requiring ten months or more of service so that attendance and participation in these workshops or institutes are compulsory and part of the teachers' contract obligations.

Teachers, supervisors, and administrators are cooperating in

---

[3] See *Rings Are Not for Resting,* American Association of School Administrators, N.E.A. (Washington, D.C.), 16 pp.

planning the courses of study, instructional procedures, and other aspects of the school program. Teachers—individually and in groups—have been given more responsibility for planning. From this has developed what has come to be known as "alternate leadership," under which not only the administrators and supervisors but also members of the teaching staff who have evidenced qualities of leadership in particular areas or particular times, are designated as temporary *ad hoc* leaders. The teaching load in such cases is adjusted to compensate for the time and energy spent on leadership or on investigation or production of activities.

Classroom visitation. In the 1930's and 1940's, most administrators and teachers felt that with few exceptions principals or supervisors should visit the classroom only upon invitation. This policy weakened their leadership. In recent years, principals and supervisors have been making more classroom visits. It should be said, however, that the classroom visit is now more friendly and is rarely of an inspectional nature. Indeed, one of the major purposes of observation is for the supervisor or the administrator to acquire the background and understanding of behavior of the youngsters under various types of conditions.

Individualized help. Supervisors and administrators are attempting to adapt leadership more definitely to the individual teacher[4] realizing that teachers vary a great deal in important characteristics which condition their effectiveness of various types of approaches. The superior teacher, the weak teacher, the teacher with unusual emotional or mental problems, the unsocial teacher, the over-confident teacher, the shy teacher—all call for different types of approaches. More supervisors and administrators are realizing this truth and are adapting their assistance to teachers to the individual.

Salaries and Ratings and Assignments

Salaries and sex. From 1940 to 1960, salaries of secondary school teachers and principals increased a little more slowly than the cost of living. Secondary school teachers' salaries in 1961–1962

---

[4] See Harl R. Douglass, Rudyard K. Bent, and Charles W. Boardman, *Democratic Supervision in Secondary Schools* (Boston, Mass.: Houghton Mifflin Co., 1961), Chapter 18.

averaged approximately $6,000, as compared to $3,365 in 1951–1952 and approximately $1,600 in 1938. In the late 1950's teachers' and principals' salaries increased even more rapidly than has the cost of living. Nevertheless, teachers' salaries since 1940 have not increased as much as has the income of individuals in other professions which require at least four years of college or university education (though beginning about 1958 the rate of increase has been as great for teachers and administrators with five or more years of college education).

TABLE 4

TRENDS IN MEDIANS OF MINIMUM AND MAXIMUM SALARIES
SCHEDULED FOR CLASSROOM TEACHERS,
1950–1951, 1958–1959, AND 1960–1961

School District, Population, and Year	TEACHERS WITH BACHELOR'S DEGREE (OR FOUR YEARS)		TEACHERS WITH MASTER'S DEGREE (OR FIVE YEARS)	
	Median of Minimums	Median of Maximums	Median of Minimums	Median of Maximums
500,000 plus				
1950–51	$2,660	$4,700	$2,863	$4,980
1958–59	4,000	6,500	4,250	6,850
1960–61	4,500	7,100	4,650	7,380
100,000–499,999				
1950–51	$2,471	$4,158	$2,656	$4,439
1958–59	4,000	6,080	4,200	6,615
1960–61	4,300	6,750	4,600	7,305
30,000–99,999				
1950–51	$2,466	$3,938	$2,652	$4,259
1958–59	4,000	6,000	4,300	6,502
1960–61	4,270	6,500	4,600	7,100
10,000–29,999				
1950–51	$2,437	$3,725	$2,608	$4,049
1958–59	3,964	5,645	4,171	6,137
1960–61	4,200	6,100	4,418	6,600
5,000–9,999				
1950–51	$2,412	$3,499	$2,567	$3,990
1958–59	3,842	5,319	4,049	5,781
1960–61	4,150	5,725	4,400	6,200
2,500–4,999				
1950–51	$2,417	$3,377	$2,556	$3,848
1958–59	3,831	5,215	4,039	5,606
1960–61	4,100	5,655	4,400	6,105

In 1960–1961 junior high school principals' average salaries in districts of from 30,000 to 100,000 population had risen to approximately $9,000; those for principals of four-year high schools, approximately $9,800 a year; and for senior high school principals, $10,000 a year.

Similar increases in salaries are found in districts of less than 30,000 and more than 100,000. In smaller districts, the salaries of the principal of six-year high schools and four-year high schools increased until the median of approximately $8,500 was reached in 1960–1961. In cities of more than 100,000, salaries of secondary school principals usually range from $7,500 to $12,500.

In 1960–1961, for the first time since 1890, a majority of secondary school teachers were men: 52.2 per cent, as compared to 45.6 per cent in 1951–1952, 35.9 per cent in 1929–1930, and 40.5 per cent in 1889–1890. This shift may be attributed largely to the increase in salaries of secondary school teachers and the much larger per cent of male teachers who complete five years preparation and therefore develop a greater stake in professional permanency.

Merit ratings. In the late 1950's there began the controversial practice of giving additional salary increases to teachers who were rated by administrators and supervisors as being definitely superior. The practice of awarding merit rating salary increases has slowly spread. In some places it seems to be operating with satisfactory results; in others it has been abandoned. In some places it does not seem to be satisfactory to a considerable number of the teachers but in some places it has been generally accepted.

There seems to be growing out of the situation a conclusion that the planning for merit rating should be a cooperative procedure in which the teachers play a prominent part and that it should not be imposed upon the teachers until they are ready to receive it. Many teachers do not have much confidence in the ratings given them by their supervisors, principals, and superintendents. It seems clear that plans for merit rating and related salary increases will have a better chance of success when the teachers play a prominent part in developing the procedure and the criteria for ratings. Also, supervisors and administrators must seriously consider the problem of arriving at ratings which are based upon the effectiveness of the teacher in promoting the educational growth of the student.

Assignments. Much attention has been given in recent years to the excessive load of the secondary school teacher, who must now spend so much more time than formerly in various types of extra-professional duties, such as serving on committees, constructing course-of-study outlines and plans, preparing and using audio-visual materials, conducting public relations and activities in the community, working with student organizations, counseling students, and conferring with parents. Particular attention has been directed to the load of the teacher of English which is commonly so great as to preclude the possibility of reading carefully the many written compositions of students.

There have been very greatly increased efforts since the mid-1950's to reduce the load of teachers not so much by decreasing the class size or in the number of class periods taught as by providing teacher aides (especially teachers of English) and assistance for mimeograph materials and audio-visual aids, and relieving him of hall duties and supervisory duties during the lunch period. Among the types of aides coming into more widespread use are: typists, clerks, parking lot attendants, multigraph and projector machine operators, library assistants, cafeteria and playground supervisors, assistants in connection with social events, and student clubs, teams, and plays.

There has been an increased effort to assign teachers only to those subject matter fields in which they have some specialized training and reasonable preparation. The increase in the size of the school, and the resulting increase of the size of the faculty, has made such efforts more successful.

The trend toward the complete departmentalized assignment of teachers in the junior high school has suffered a reverse in recent years. There has developed the feeling that boys and girls in the seventh grade should be taught at least two subjects (and probably three for the first semester) by the same teacher and that students should be taught two subjects by the same teacher in the eighth grade.

In many schools team teaching results in a greater fragmentation of the area to which teachers are assigned, since several teachers assist in teaching one course, each taking over the field or the instruction activities in which he is specialized or superior.

Professionalization

In recent years the career of teaching has more nearly approached professional status. In spite of wishful thinking on the part of teachers, there are some aspects of professional status which have not been clearly attained. Since 1945 there has been a noticeable trend for teachers to stay in the profession longer, probably as the result of the increased amount of time and money invested in preparation for secondary school teaching, the increases in salaries, and in the improved status of teachers in the community.

The increase in the preparation of teachers to five years contributes to more definite recognition of teaching as a profession and to rendering a high-level specialized service.

Another evidence of greater professionalization is a steady trend toward increased enrollment in national and state professional organizations of various types and the increased amount of money that is spent for professional reading material.

Teacher Load

Teachers' loads have increased in the past twenty-five years. The class period has lengthened. The time needed for adequate preparation in modern teaching is greater. In the past decade, the load of many teachers has been lightened by such devices as aides who assist in reading papers, working with individual students, and clerical personnel who help to relieve teachers of cutting stencils, assembling duplicated work, filing, preparing audio-visual materials, assist in laboratories, home-economics units, and shop.

BIBLIOGRAPHY

Hadenfield, B. K., and T. M. Stinnett. *The Education of Teachers—Conflicts and Consensus.* (Englewood Cliffs, N.J.: Prentice-Hall, Inc., 1961.)

Horrocks, John E., and Thelma I. Schoonover, "Self-Evaluation as a Means of Growth for Teachers in Service: Use of a Self-Analysis Questionnaire," *Educational Administration and Supervision*, Vol. 36, No. 2 (February, 1950), pp. 83–90.

Lawrence, Noel, "In-Service Programs for High School Teachers," *Educational Leadership*, Vol. 17 (March, 1960), pp. 344–46.

Logan, Edgar, "The Rutgers Plan for Teaching English" (the use of assistants), *Saturday Review,* Vol. 64 (August 19, 1961), pp. 42–3, 49.

Mitchum, P. M., *The High School Principal and Staff Plan for Program Improvement.* New York: Columbia University Press, 1958, 111 pp.

Olson, A. R., "Organizing a Faculty for Curriculum Improvement," *The Bulletin of the N.A.S.S.P.,* No. 253 (February, 1960), pp. 94–8.

Polatnick, Samuel, "A High School Faculty Looks at Secondary Education," *The Bulletin of the N.A.S.S.P.,* No. 229 (September, 1958), pp. 112–18.

Stirling, Thomas, and Lerue Winger, "What is the Case *For* and *Against* Merit Rating for Teachers?" *The Bulletin of the N.A.S.S.P.,* No. 255 (April, 1960), pp. 92–5.

Index

Index